ABOUT ISLAND PRESS

Island Press is the only nonprofit organization in the United States whose principal purpose is the publication of books on environmental issues and natural resource management. We provide solutions-oriented information to professionals, public officials, business and community leaders, and concerned citizens who are shaping responses to environmental problems.

In 2004, Island Press celebrates its twentieth anniversary as the leading provider of timely and practical books that take a multidisciplinary approach to critical environmental concerns. Our growing list of titles reflects our commitment to bringing the best of an expanding body of literature to the environmental community throughout North America and the world.

Support for Island Press is provided by the Agua Fund, Brainerd Foundation, Geraldine R. Dodge Foundation, Doris Duke Charitable Foundation, Educational Foundation of America, The Ford Foundation, The George Gund Foundation, The William and Flora Hewlett Foundation, Henry Luce Foundation, The John D. and Catherine T. MacArthur Foundation, The Andrew W. Mellon Foundation, The Curtis and Edith Munson Foundation, National Environmental Trust, The New-Land Foundation, Oak Foundation, The Overbrook Foundation, The David and Lucile Packard Foundation, The Pew Charitable Trusts, The Rockefeller Foundation, The Winslow Foundation, and other generous donors.

The opinions expressed in this book are those of the author(s) and do not necessarily reflect the views of these foundations.

KEEPERS OF THE SPRING

KEEPERS OF THE SPRING

RECLAIMING

OUR WATER

IN AN AGE OF

GLOBALIZATION

FRED PEARCE

ISLAND PRESS

WASHINGTON ☐ COVELO ☐ LONDON

Library of Congress Cataloging-in-Publication data.

Pearce, Fred.
  Keepers of the spring : reclaiming our water in an age of globalization / Fred Pearce.
    p. cm.
  Includes bibliographical references and index.
  ISBN 1-55963-681-5 (cloth : alk. paper)
  1. Water-supply—Management. 2. Water-supply—History. 3. Water conservation. I. Title.
  TD345.P33 2004
  333.91—dc22

                            2004012079

British Cataloguing-in-Publication data available.

Printed on recycled, acid-free paper ✪

Design by Kathleen Szawiola

Manufactured in the United States of America
10 9 8 7 6 5 4 3 2 1

TO THE MEMORY OF ANIL AGARWAL

CONTENTS

15   The People's Green Revolution   173

16   Trickles and Floods   181

17   Making Water from Thin Air   195

18   Restoring African Hydrology   207

19   Reviving the Wetlands   221

CONCLUSION

20   Battle for the New Agenda   233

      Further Readings   249
      Acknowledgments   253
      Index   255

PART I

Riding the Water Cycle

Introduction

Buried beneath the hills west of Jerusalem, there is a secret that many Palestinians have forgotten and many Jews never knew but that unites the two communities in a long history of water use in the Holy Land. Zvi Ron, a geographer from Tel Aviv, discovered that secret one day when he dropped his glasses down a chimneylike hole that he had noticed near some agricultural terraces he was mapping. It was a second or so before his glasses hit hard rock. Even though the lenses were smashed, he decided to go in after them.

Armed with a strong flashlight, he found not just a deep hole, but a long tunnel extending from it. It was big enough for him to walk along. It had neatly quarried sides and stone slabs for a roof. After several dozen yards, it ended in a large excavated cavern where water dripped slowly from the rock and trickled into a channel on the floor. The water, it seemed, found its way along the tunnels and came out on the terraces where vegetables and oranges were growing—the same ones he had been surveying.

What Ron had discovered that day was only one of many dozens of man-made tunnels in the dolomite hills near Jerusalem, west toward Tel Aviv, north onto the West Bank, and south toward the Dead Sea. Palestine,

Israel, the Holy Land—whatever you choose to call it—is honeycombed with these tunnels tapping underground water sources to bring water to the arid surface. After discovering that few written records acknowledged the existence of these tunnels, and that few people even among the locals were aware they existed, Ron has laboriously mapped most of them in the 30 years since he lost his glasses.

The few historical records that exist suggest that most of these tunnels are an extraordinary engineering legacy that is at least 2,000 years old. They have watered the traditional terraces of Palestinians, Jews, and the many other communities that have lived in these lands during that time. The villages of Artus, Battir, Zova, Abu Ghosh, and dozens of others relied on them. More strangely, these indigenous water sources have often been replaced since the Israelis returned here in 1948, with water piped for tens of miles from distant boreholes and even the Sea of Galilee far to the north. In many places, the old terraces that the tunnels once watered are also long gone, replaced by the flat fields and mechanized farming of modern Israeli kibbutzim. But the tunnels remain, hidden underground. Some are empty now—deprived of supply as underground water levels across the area have fallen. Others are still directing water. But almost all lie abandoned. And their locations and purposes, and even existence, are known to an ever diminishing band.

I joined Ron on a day of discovery beneath the hills. We went first to a tunnel 4 miles west of Jerusalem close to Zova, a Palestinian village that was emptied in 1948 and replaced by an Israeli kibbutz of the same name. Switching on his miner's lamp, Ron, who works at the University of Tel Aviv, led me down a shaft beneath the grass. We entered a dark, dank cavern, a collecting room for water, from which a series of tunnels headed off in different directions. Some burrowed ever deeper into the hills; others headed toward the surface, where until half a century ago Palestinians used the water to irrigate vegetable plots and water orange groves. Everywhere, expertly, the unknown excavators of the Zova tunnels had ensured that the water could flow along a shallow gradient beneath sloping hillsides, from the hidden water reserves to the fields.

The Zova cavern, like most of the tunnels beneath these hills, is largely unknown except to the dwindling bands of Palestinians who have farmed here and a few inquisitive souls like Ron. Ron calls them spring-flow tunnels. Their excavators made them by following the route of the spring waters back into the rocks. They found that by constructing these tunnels they could increase the flow of the springs and make sporadic seasonal sources of water into permanent streams. "These spring tunnels are technological masterpieces," Ron says in awe.

Some Palestinians insist that the tunnels are an indigenous Arab technology. Many historians say the idea came from Persia. But Ron believes that many were dug by Jewish communities before his people were thrown out of the Holy Land by the Romans. Clearly, this is a politically charged debate. But archaeological evidence certainly seems to point to the excavation of the spring-flow tunnels perhaps around 2,000 years ago, when Jews fought Romans in these hills. One tunnel, for instance, lies beneath a monastery at Abu Ghosh, a bustling and picturesque Palestinian village overlooking Jerusalem. The monastery was a Crusader church in the twelfth century, and legend has it the Ark of the Covenant was once stored here. French surveyors renovating the monastery a century ago assumed that the tunnel had been an escape route to the surrounding fields for Crusaders in case of a siege. But the tunnel is clearly older than that. And further excavation shows that it supplies water to a crypt that was used as a water reservoir by the Romans.

Whoever first developed it, the tunneling technology used in these hills clearly has great antiquity. One of the ancient world's oldest hard-rock tunnels is the Siloam Tunnel, on the outskirts of old Jerusalem. It took water from a secret spring outside the city walls, known as the Gihon Spring, through a 500-yard tunnel to a reservoir in the heart of the ancient City of David. Long-standing Jewish claims hold that it was the tunnel mentioned in the Bible as being built around 700 BC by King Hezekiah as a protection against siege. Those claims were confirmed in 2003 through radiocarbon dating.

Though the evidence suggests that Jews first excavated at least some of the spring-flow tunnels, it is the Palestinians who in more recent times have used and maintained them. A few dozen still irrigate fields or supplement village water supplies. In the West Bank village of Madama, near Nablus, I met Ahmad Qot, a poor Palestinian who every day walks his donkey to collect water from a spring tunnel that delivers water from the hills above to the heart of the village.

At Battir, a village of 3,000 Palestinians in a gorge near Bethlehem, eight Palestinian clans continued to take water from a spring-flow tunnel until the 1980s, using it to irrigate vegetables and fill pitchers for their homes. Each clan could take water in turn, once every eight days, according to an ancient tradition of water sharing. An elder of the village measured the daily ration by putting a notched stick into the tunnel's reservoir and opening a sluice gate to divert water until the water level had fallen by one notch on the stick.

This ritual may have been carried on by Jew and Palestinian alike since the second century, when Battir was the last Jewish fortress to fall to Roman conquerors. Today the village is in the shadow of two huge Jewish settlements and as a result has been in the front line of the intifada. The villagers fight what they see as a settlers' invasion of their land. The spring tunnel still discharges water, but the ancient clan sharing system has broken down, and the water is now conveyed to a storage pond through a metal pipe.

Most of the tunnels near Jerusalem were abandoned when half a million Palestinians fled their fields and orchards in 1948 after the creation of the Jewish state of Israel. Ron calls his people's ignorance of this water-collecting system a tragedy, and it certainly proved a hydrological step backward for many areas. The new occupants at Zova, for instance, brought in tractors to build a kibbutz. In the process, they unknowingly destroyed parts of the ancient spring tunnels. And, unaware of the resource on its doorstep, the kibbutz ended up taking its irrigation water from springs 20 miles away. Such stories have been repeated all across the former Palestinian lands.

Across the hills of the West Bank, Ron has mapped more than 250 abandoned spring-flow tunnels. "The majority are hidden, with only small, dark openings. Perhaps if any researchers knew about them, they didn't mention them because they were afraid to enter them," he muses.

Close to the main road between Tel Aviv and Jerusalem, beneath a ridge where thousands of factory hens let out a constant screech, Ron took me to visit the village of Ein Khandaq, which Palestinians describe as having been "ethnically cleansed" in 1948. Here there is a spring-flow tunnel from which water bubbles up into a small reservoir and then pours down a series of channels and waterfalls to irrigate stone-walled fields arranged in a shallow flight down the valley. This immaculately designed irrigation system still pours its water into the fields, even though the fields have not been cultivated for more than half a century. The system's only visitors are curious schoolchildren and a part-time caretaker.

"Ein Khandaq shows real hydrological knowledge," says Ron, who was the first Israeli to explore it. "It was designed as an entire system." The reservoir overflows into channels at a point some 6 feet above the level at which water enters it from the tunnel behind. This allows it to irrigate the topmost terraces without reducing the flow from the spring. Its designers had exquisite knowledge of what they were doing, or they could not have come up with this configuration as the optimum solution to irrigating the terraces below. They knew, says Ron, the mathematical relationship between water height and the flow it would produce. "Modern hydrologists know this relationship as Darcy's law," he says, after the French engineer Henri Darcy, who discovered it in 1856. It is one of the cornerstones of modern hydrology. "But whoever built this system, however many centuries ago, obviously figured out the law long before Darcy. They didn't make this up as they went along. They had to design the whole thing before they could begin digging." Even now, after visiting the site many times, Ron stands open-mouthed, with a scientist's sense of wonder at the achievement.

■ How could such expertise, such scientific skill and engineering prowess be lost? There are, of course, special circumstances in the Middle East. When the state of Israel was established, the new bosses across these hills had new ideas about introducing modern mechanized farming. They preferred flat fields operated by mechanized equipment to tiny terraces. They preferred pumps and boreholes to the vagaries of the spring tunnels. And they acted on their beliefs, even if that meant ignoring local water sources and bringing water halfway across the country in the National Water Carrier, a distribution pipeline supplied mainly by the Sea of Galilee.

On the West Bank, the repercussions of that change are very clear. Most of the West Bank water ends up in Israeli hands. Israelis have the power to stop new wells being dug in Palestinian villages. Some 80 percent of the water that falls as rain onto the West Bank is now taken by Israeli pumps. The per capita water consumption of the Israeli community is four times greater than that of the Palestinians.

But Israel is not unique. What has happened here is an acute and politically charged version of what has been happening around the world as traditional water-gathering methods—many of which now seem to modern eyes almost like the mysteries of water divining—have given way to modern industrialized and centralized ways of water collection and distribution.

Such growing water inequality is typical even of areas without political and social disharmony. The cause of that inequality lies as much in the choice of technology for water capture and distribution as it does in power politics and ethnic division. Everywhere large projects—many of them hydrologically inefficient, inequitable, and ill-conceived—are swamping smaller, more efficient, more equitable, and more practical water supply systems.

Ironically, the most ambitious of these projects are being built to satisfy the demands of growing populations for clean, secure water sources. Those who oppose them cite their impacts on ecosystems and displacement of people. But perhaps the most compelling argument against the massive projects now under way is that they probably will not work. They may be built, but they are unlikely to produce the advertised benefits. As Part II of this book demonstrates, the recent history of these massive civil engineering projects reveals outcomes ranging from merely disappointing to catastrophic. In some places, the most tragic aspect of these projects is that they displace older, more efficient technologies that had served their inventors well for centuries.

And yet, in some places, almost at the moment of being extinguished, the small water technologies are reviving and offering an alternative way forward—a way that may prove more sustainable not just for the environment but also for those billions of people who still lack adequate water supplies to irrigate their crops and fill their domestic taps. Part III of this book will spend time seeking out those experiments and assessing their potential. We'll visit places as arid as the Chihuahua desert, as impoverished as sub-Saharan Africa, and as crowded as the Indian subcontinent to explore these new and rediscovered technologies and the people, the keepers of the spring, who are making them work.

No one technology, or suite of technologies, can do the job alone, however. Ultimately, we may need to rethink our approach to water management. Among the hallmarks of the successful water projects of the past is that built into them is a water ethic, one that encourages the careful allocation and use of water as community property, property on which the survival of entire peoples depended. Ultimately, this book explores the possibility of drawing on these ancient traditions to create a new water ethic for the twenty-first century. In a very real sense, we must all become keepers of the spring if we are to survive the water crises that await us.

If the twentieth century was the era of the megadam and the canalization and ecological destruction of the world's rivers, of emptying underground water reserves, and of the pollution of many of those that remain, then the twenty-first century could be different. It could. But will it? First, we look at the people who continue to believe that, in the world of water at least, big is beautiful.

CHAPTER ONE

Megawater

In a modest ceremony in Beijing in April 2003, a small bottle of water was presented to the city's vice-mayor, Niu Youcheng. To an outsider it didn't seem like much—a variant on some ancient Chinese tea ceremony, perhaps. But its significance for the future of a city of 14 million people, the capital of the world's largest country, could be profound. The water had come from the Danjiangkou Reservoir, a huge man-made expanse of water more than 600 miles away to the south, on a tributary of the River Yangtze, the world's fourth-largest river. Its arrival in Beijing symbolized the start of what China is calling the biggest engineering project ever undertaken anywhere on the planet. It is a scheme to divert part of the flow of the Yangtze, which drains most of southern China, to replenish the parched north, where rising demand for water for farms and cities is emptying the Yellow River, and where underground waters on which cities like Beijing increasingly rely are being pumped dry.

The first Yangtze water should be flowing north along a canal from Danjiangkou in time for Beijing to fill swimming pools and festoon its stadiums with fountains during the Olympic Games, which it is scheduled to host in 2008. The canal will be 200 feet wide and as long as France, crossing 219 rivers, 500 roads, and 120 railway lines as it takes some 10 million acre-feet of water a year across the crowded plains en route to Beijing. To provide this extra water the Danjiangkou Reservoir, already Asia's widest artificial expanse of freshwater, will be raised to 550 feet, displacing a quarter-million people.

But this is just one of three links planned to bring water from the Yangtze to the great cities and wheat fields of northern China. It will be complemented by two other equally large and complex diversions, one to the east and another far to the west in Tibet. By the time all three stages of what China calls the south-north diversion are completed in around 20 years, the project will be siphoning north around 40 million acre-feet of water a year. That is less than a tenth of the Yangtze's typical annual flow, but almost equivalent to the current flow of the Yellow River in its middle reaches and approaching three times what it discharges into the sea in a typical year.

This is big engineering. Chinese engineers are still imbued with a sense of optimism about their ability to remake the landscape—an optimism that has largely been lost in the West. They are attempting nothing less than the replumbing of their nation by remaking two of the world's greatest rivers. The south-to-north project follows hot on the heels of the Three Gorges Dam, whose reservoir is already being filled on the Yangtze. Three Gorges will be the world's largest hydroelectric dam and will create a lake some 250 miles long. But it suddenly seems like a warm-up act for the main event, whose three stages will each match the Three Gorges for size and cost. It is as if the United States decided to dam the Mississippi at Minneapolis, at St. Louis, and again at Memphis and to pipe its waters into the Rockies to refill the Colorado. The implications are immense.

The eastern arm of this vast undertaking will extract water from near the mouth of the Yangtze and pour it into the 1,500-year-old Grand Canal. This wonder of ancient China was the largest artificial river of the preindustrial world and the first to have lock gates. It was built primarily to transport rice from the wet south of the country to the north. At one stage, it carried 400,000 tons of rice a year, helping feed an army of more than a million soldiers camped in the north to repel barbarians. But today much of it is a foul-smelling sump for China's rampant industrialization. The plan is to clean it and use the ancient waterway as a conduit to bring north the precious Yangtze water, take it beneath the bed of the Yellow River and onto the North China Plain, China's breadbasket, where it will serve the 10 million inhabitants of the water-starved city of Tianjin.

The third, western, arm of the south-north diversion will also be the biggest and most complex. It will capture the headwaters of the Yangtze behind a 1,000-foot-high dam amid the melting glaciers of Tibet. It will then lift a volume of water equivalent to a quarter of the flow of the River Nile through a 70-mile tunnel into the upper reaches of the Yellow River. Construction of this final link is due to start around 2010. All told, the south-north transfer scheme will cost at least $60 billion.

Until now, the world has largely built its cities where the water is— close to big rivers. Even modern superdams like the Hoover Dam, the Aswan on the Nile, and the Soviet-built monstrosities perched in the quake-infested mountains of Central Asia usually do little more than control the flow of their rivers. They catch seasonal floods in the mountains and release them downstream in the dry season, or they divert water to irrigate the plains of the river's own basin. But China's south-north project is something different. It aims to move water on a huge scale to where the people are. Indeed, to where several hundred million people are.

According to the country's water lords, China has no choice but to embark on such breathtaking plumbing. As Wang Hao of the China Institute of Water Resources in Beijing told me in early 2003, his country is suffering "a hydrological crisis that threatens the nation's future." Five times in the previous decade, the 3,000-mile-long Yellow River had failed to reach the sea for part of the year. In 1997, its lower reaches were dry for more than 200 days. Every last drop had been removed to fill irrigation channels and city taps. Parts of the river's parched upper basin are turning to desert, unleashing dust storms of such ferocity that a yellowish haze is still in the air when the winds from China finally turn up a week later across the Pacific Ocean in western Canada. As Wang outlined his plans to me, the river had just recorded its lowest spring flow for 50 years. Irrigation channels intended to water the wheat fields across 40 million acres of northern China had dried up.

In recent years, Chinese farmers and urban authorities alike have increasingly given up on the Yellow River and turned instead to pumping out ancient reserves of underground water in the sediments beneath the riverbed and across the wider plains of northern China. But these reserves themselves depend to a considerable extent on the river's flow for replenishment. During times of flood especially, water seeps downward from the riverbed. Low river flow means no replenishment. And not surprisingly, with replenishment down and pumping at record levels, the underground water also is running out. The water table beneath Beijing has fallen 200 feet in the last 40 years. In places near the city, 90 percent of the underground water reserve is gone. And once the groundwaters become depleted, water tables are too low for them to top up the river during the dry season. The entire Yellow River basin enters a vicious cycle of aridification.

The north of China, which has two-thirds of the country's cropland but only a fifth of the water, is estimated to be pumping from beneath the ground as much as 25 million acre-feet more water each year than rain and the river can replenish. And Wang's institute predicts that water demand in the basin could increase by a further 30 million acre-feet a year by 2030, making a vast annual deficit of 55 million acre-feet a year. At that rate, even two Yellow Rivers would not be enough to feed northern China's predicted needs.

For China's water engineers and politicians this state of affairs can be turned around only by radically altering the country's hydrology. The monsoon lands of the south will have to come to the rescue of the dry north. Dominated by the Yangtze, southern China has four-fifths of the country's water but only a third of its fields. Rice paddies soak up a fair amount of this water. But still more than 90 percent of the Yangtze's flows, which have always dwarfed those of the Yellow River, pour into the sea. And sometimes they take embarrassing detours onto the land first. In 1998, there were floods on the Yangtze. A quarter of a billion people fled its waters in what was probably the largest human evacuation in history. Some 3,000 people drowned. Many feared a repeat of previous flood disasters in 1954, in which some 30,000 people perished. So, given the surplus of water in the south, what could be more natural than to pipe the Yangtze's excess water north? We will return later to answer that question, but Chinese water engineers regard it as entirely rhetorical. The answer is obvious, they say. There is nothing more natural, and it should be done.

While China may be the first to act on such a scale, it is not alone in harboring such plans. National and international replumbing is the new vogue among engineers, for whom mere dam building has become passé. A rash of similar megaprojects—the pipedreams of engineers and geopoliticians around the world for many years—are on the verge of being turned into reality. Serious plans and serious funding are being assembled for schemes in the mountains of Spain, on the parched plains of India, in the Western Desert of Egypt, and maybe soon in the Australian outback, in the jungles of central Africa, and amid the icy torrents of northern Canada. All aim to cut civilizations loose from their geography, to bring water long-distance to where the people are—or where their leaders wish them to be.

■   Is all this mega-engineering the inevitable future? Will the twenty-first century be the era of national water grids and planetary replumbing in the way that the twentieth century became the era of blockading rivers with dams? A handful of small, arid countries, most notably Israel and Libya, already pump most of their water down pipes that cross watersheds between river basins. So does California. Will larger nations now follow?

The world undoubtedly faces a growing crisis over its management of water. Besides the Yellow River, other great world rivers such as the Indus in Pakistan; the Colorado and the Rio Grande, both shared by the United States and Mexico; and the Nile, which is shared by a dozen countries through East Africa, have all periodically run empty in recent years because humans have abstracted their every last drop. Meanwhile, underground water sometimes tens of thousands of years old is being "mined" in several countries. By some estimates, the world's farmers are pumping out 160 million acre-feet per year more water from underground than is being restored by rains and rivers. As a result, water tables are crashing, and pumping bills are soaring.

Economists increasingly see water supply as a critical constraint on economic development. The World Bank predicts that by 2025, water scarcity will be cutting global food production by 350 million tons a year. That is the equivalent of a loaf of bread every week for every person on the planet. Yet amid concern about finding water to irrigate crops, even the basic human need for clean water for drinking is not being met. More than a billion people in shanty towns and remote villages across the developing world have no access to reliably clean drinking water. The World Summit on Sustainable Development in Johannesburg in 2002 promised to halve that figure by 2015. But to do so will require making new water connections to 125,000 people every day. And even if the pipes can be laid, nobody is sure where the water will come from. The summit also promised to bring modern sanitation to more than a billion people. But that too will require water to flush the toilets and empty the pipes.

On current trends, by 2025 more than 2 billion people will be living in regions of the world that are seriously short of water. So it is hardly surprising that politicians in China, India, Pakistan, Egypt, and other heavily populated and water-stressed countries want their water engineers to come up with solutions—and fast. And if that means bringing water in from distant regions where there is spare water, then so be it. To politicians big engineering seems not just beautiful but essential, even though it is also a potential cause of international disputes. Yet still many believe that the heyday of giant water projects is over, that they can no longer deliver on their promises.

One strand of this argument holds that a world of mega water engineering is too dangerous because it will trigger water wars. Most of the world's great rivers cross borders. Almost half the world's population lives in an international river basin. The Danube, Rhine, Congo, Nile, Niger, and Zambezi Rivers all pass through nine or more nations. Two-thirds of international river basins have no treaties for sharing their water. Each is the source of a potential water war. Already, water disputes are a major source of tension between nations. They create trouble between India and Pakistan; Israel and its neighbors; Syria and Turkey; and India (again) and Bangladesh, to name but a few. And all the while global warming is altering rainfall patterns, rates of glacial melting, and river flows in ways that increase the risks of drought and flood—and of water disputes. The River Indus, already one of the most vital, intensely used, and hotly disputed rivers in the world, could lose 40 percent of its annual flow within half a century according to some estimates.

Another strand holds simply that even with world hydrological peace, mega-engineering is part of the problem rather than part of the solution. "Past approaches no longer seem sufficient," says one of the world's leading authorities on water management, Peter Gleick of the Pacific Institute for Studies in Development, Environment and Security in Oakland, California. While big engineering undoubtedly brought benefits for hundreds of millions, particularly in cities, during the twentieth century, it also had "substantial and often unanticipated social, economic, and environmental costs," he says, especially among the rural poor. In addition to the tens of millions of people who lost their homes and livelihoods directly to flooding from large dams and other water infrastructure projects, there are hundreds of millions who lost fisheries, flood irrigation, silt, and the many ecological services provided by rivers on their floodplains and beyond.

Environmentalists point out that diverting river waters away from their basins and into entirely new and often distant catchments will create a whole new suite of problems. Dams are already largely responsible for dramatic declines in the world's freshwater fisheries, but transfers between basins will further destabilize ecosystems and shift predator species and diseases from one river system to another. Many point to the appalling ecological havoc in Central Asia when Russian engineers diverted most of the flows of two giant rivers away from the Aral Sea catchment onto a vast irrigated landscape of cotton fields. The Aral Sea has dried up, turning the surrounding area into a salt-encrusted and toxic wilderness.

Moreover, during the twentieth century, most of the immediately attractive water schemes, the ones that produce the most for the least cost, were completed. The best dam sites are already plugged. Future projects will deliver less and at greater financial, social, and environmental cost.

So, before we start writing the billion-dollar checks, it is worth considering if there is another, cheaper, and better way. The need now, according to Gleick, is for a "soft path" that complements centralized physical infrastructure with lower-cost community-scale systems, efficient technology, and environmental protection. People like Gleick argue that we have got the nature of our current water crisis all wrong. We are not running out of water. What we face is a crisis about how we use and manage water. We do not have a supply-side problem so much as a demand-side problem. The bottom line is that we manage water so badly now that the potential for doing it better is vast. The solution in most cases is not more and bigger engineering schemes. We have to treat nature as the ultimate provider of water, rather than its wasteful withholder. We must learn to "ride the water cycle."

There are really two "soft" solutions. The first is to devise new ways of collecting water locally. In many arid regions, there is ample rain, but it all falls during a few stormy days and rapidly runs off the land and away into rivers and the sea. In monsoon lands like India, all the rain falls in around a hundred hours a year. What is needed in such places is a revival of local systems for collecting the rain, either storing it in tanks or allowing it to percolate into the soil, from where it can be pumped up later.

The second "soft" solution is to make more sensible use of the water that has been collected. Using water more efficiently could drastically lessen the need for more dams and water transfers. In the United States, the amount of water used to flush the nation's toilets has been cut by three-quarters in the past two decades, thanks to some fairly modest alterations to the design of toilets. Similar savings can be made by redesigning everything from shower units and public urinals to industrial processes.

The biggest savings can undoubtedly be made in agriculture, the most expansive economic activity on the planet and also the largest consumer of water. In the United States, farmers used roughly 50 trillion gallons of water in 2000, about one-third of the country's total water use. Most of that water use is in relatively efficient irrigation systems (though there is vast room for improvement). But from Spain to northern China, Mexico to Morocco, most farmers still irrigate crops by flooding their fields, when the job could be done far more efficiently with drips from a perforated hose. Further savings can be made by leveling the land, changing to water-efficient plant varieties, and using water-saving cropping methods such as direct-seeding rice, planting along furrows, and reducing tilling. At present, only around 1 percent of the world's irrigated farms use such methods. Even in a severely water-stressed country like China the figure is only 3 percent. As a result, at a conservative estimate, two-thirds of the water sent down irrigation canals never reaches the plants it is intended for.

There is similar scope for making savings in supply systems. Evaporation from the surfaces of reservoirs can be dramatically cut simply by using polymer solutions spread on the water surface. That could significantly improve the efficiency of reservoirs, from the Colorado to the Nile. In cities from London to Nairobi, between a third and a half of all the water put into urban water mains disappears through leaks before reaching its customers. Yet cities with leak management programs have found cost-effective ways of saving huge amounts of water. Singapore has got its leaks down to 5 percent.

The scope for savings is often greatest in the driest, most water-stressed nations. Countries like Mexico and Morocco, Pakistan and Uzbekistan have the highest per capita water demands in the world, far exceeding those of more developed and urbanized countries in temperate lands, where crops need little if any irrigation and can rely on the rains most years. Egypt, for instance, which has to irrigate all its crops, uses five times more water per capita than Switzerland. But less than half the water so expensively collected, transported, and supplied to farmers' fields currently reaches the crops. The rest is lost to evaporation and seepage.

Humanity now uses more than a quarter of the water that falls to the ground in rain. We are reaching the practical limit of supply; solutions lie in better demand management. Even modest efforts at using water more efficiently would end the world water crisis. In most places, we can fill the taps without emptying the rivers.

Many believe with Gleick that we require a "new water ethic"—one based not on meeting water shortages with supply-side solutions and confronting nature with our inflated demands for water, but on water saving and respect for the environmental services provided by the natural water cycle. This would be going with the grain of developments in other areas once dominated by technocratic solutions. The theory is that we will one day save water in the way we are learning to save energy and recycle waste—for the good of our planet as well as our pockets. And, were we to adopt such an ethic, we would increasingly look for local solutions to our problems, rather than attempting to replumb the planet. It remains to be seen if we will be able to do so.

■ Why do we nonetheless remain so fixated with giant water projects? Large engineering companies and state enterprises love the big contracts, of course. But we, the public, also yearn for large and simple solutions to large and complex problems. And these hankerings help to make big, prestige projects popular with governments. While such projects are being built, politicians can bask in the credit for taking bold action to solve a national problem. When the projects are finished, the politicians get to put their names on the structures. From the Hoover Dam in the United States to the Indira Gandhi Canal in India and Lake Nasser in Egypt, big hydrology projects commemorate their political champions. By the time recriminations start to fly over technical problems, ecological calamities, and cost overruns, the politicians responsible are usually out of office.

Megaprojects become national fantasies. Every twentieth-century nation wanted its Hoover Dam, its concrete temple to the modern world. Every arid nation wanted to exert its will to "green the desert." Water planners continue to collude in this process by assuming that water demand will rise as it has in the past. "Planners consistently assume continued and even accelerating exponential growth in total water demand," says Gleick, whereas in some countries, at least, water demand has ceased to rise. U.S. water demand, for instance, is actually lower today than in the early 1980s, and the economic productivity of American water has doubled.

At the Third World Water Forum, held in Kyoto, Japan, in 2003, governments signed up to the notion, put to them by engineers, that investment in water infrastructure worldwide needed to rise to a staggering $200 billion every year by 2025. But as Gleick points out, "This figure is based on the assumption that future global water demand will reach the level of industrialized nations and that centralized and expensive water supply and treatment infrastructure will have to provide it."

If the engineers have their way, soon every nation will want not just large dams and vast irrigation projects, but also water transfer schemes— south to north, east to west, up hill and down dale they will run.

CHAPTER TWO

Hydraulic Civilizations

It begins with a few wispy clouds in the clear blue equatorial skies over the Indian Ocean. Soon the winds turn north, bearing water vapor that has evaporated from the ocean. The clouds grow. The water droplets slowly coalesce within the clouds. Eventually the skies darken, thunder claps, and the first giant drops of rain fall on the southern tip of India. The monsoon has begun, and the clouds will sweep north across the subcontinent, enveloping it in curtains of rain and bringing a parched and overheated land back to life. The drenching will be brief but complete. In about a hundred hours, spread across fewer than a hundred days, millions of communities across India will receive virtually all the rain they will get for the coming year. The rain will swell rivers, flood low-lying land, fill reservoirs, turn deserts green, bring crops to life, and percolate through saturated soils to fill giant underground reserves in porous rocks. In the Himalayas, the rain will combine with melting waters from ancient glaciers to feed the country's great northern rivers like the Ganges and the Brahmaputra.

As the first rains come, Indians rush out into the streets, party, and put on festivals for their Hindu water gods. They head for the fields to plant crops in soil that has turned from dust to mud in a few hours. They clear debris from ancient channels that divert the precious rains into ponds and lakes that store water through the year. In some places, they even pour the rains down into their wells for safekeeping. The ritual of the monsoon is repeated, a few weeks earlier or later, across most of Asia. At the same time, in the Americas, farmers watch the skies, waiting for the tropical storms that grow in the Caribbean before breaking droughts in Central America and bringing the first hurricanes of the season to the United States.

Western, eastern, and southern Africa, too, all have their own monsoons. These are a matter of life and death for hundreds of millions of the continent's poorest people. If the rains fail, many will die. Too much, and many will be washed away in floods. Outside the rainy season, months go by without a drop falling from the sky. The capture and efficient storage of the precious liquid has been vital to human survival since time immemorial. No human can live for more than five days without water. It is more valuable than oil, more vital than food, and yet is often taken for granted until it is not there. As Benjamin Franklin once put it: "When the well's dry, we know the worth of water."

■ No wonder that the first rains are a time of hope and renewal. Our water is constantly being renewed and cleansed by nature. Those clouds forming over the Indian Ocean are one step in a never-ending water cycle. Water that evaporates from the oceans accumulates in the atmosphere until it collects into clouds and, when the water droplets in the clouds get big enough, falls as rain. Once on the ground, the water may get tied up in plants or consumed by humans or other animals; it may flow off the land into rivers and back to the sea; or it may freeze in ice caps or disappear underground, for periods that can last from days to millions of years, before seeping into the oceans or returning to the surface.

This basic water cycle has persisted for eons. The water we drink today is the same water that froze during the ice ages and boiled when an asteroid hit the oceans 65 million years ago, the same water in which the first fish swam and the first dinosaurs bathed. Our planet probably has no more and no less of it than it has had for most of its history. Nature endlessly recycles it. Each day around the Earth some 650 million acre-feet of water—ten times the annual flow of the River Nile—evaporate from the oceans and forests and grasslands and form a thin mist of water vapor in the atmosphere. On average, 10 days later—though it could be hours or months—that water vapor condenses to form cloud droplets and then falls as rain.

From there some of the water is taken up by plants; some percolates down through soils to natural underground reservoirs in the pores of rocks, where it may stay for a few weeks or tens of thousands of years; some pours down rivers and into the oceans; and increasing amounts are captured by humans for filling taps, irrigating crops, incorporating into industrial processes, or squirting through hydroelectric turbines before the precious liquid is returned to nature. But wherever the water temporarily resides, it will, sooner or later, return to the sky as the sun evaporates it once more. The water cycle is complete.

The Earth is the water planet. It contains an almost unimaginable 1,134 trillion acre-feet of the stuff. But more than 95 percent of this is salty seawater that we cannot drink and cannot, except in very local circumstances, afford to purify. In practice, only a minute fraction of the water on our planet is fit and ready for our use at any one time. Of the remaining freshwater, four-fifths is locked up in ice caps and glaciers, mostly for centuries or millennia. After that we are in luck. But even then, around 95 percent of the world's liquid freshwater is stored underground. Much of it has been there for hundreds or even thousands of years. However, with the expenditure of sufficient energy, we can pump it to the surface, and, with important exceptions that we will discuss in Chapter 8, it is usually clean and safe to drink. The rest is already at the surface, in lakes and soils and atmospheric water vapor and living organisms and—just 1 percent of all the surface water at any one time—in our rivers. Even the greatest torrents like the River Amazon, between whose mighty banks a fifth of all the world's river water flows, are mere splashes in the planetary bucket.

Most settlements across the world are built beside rivers, because easily accessible water is the first requirement of every community. But nature in her perversity has placed many of the world's greatest rivers in regions of the planet where few people can or want to live. The Amazon Basin, mostly comprising thick rain forest on top of thin, sterile soils, is one of the least populated regions on the planet. The next two largest rivers in terms of annual water flow—the Congo in central Africa and the Amazon's neighbor, the north-flowing Orinoco—likewise drain thick jungle. And three more of the top-ten biggest rivers—the Lena and Yenisei in Siberia and the Mackenzie in northern Canada—run mostly through Arctic wastes.

The roll call of the world's most watery places is largely a reminder of the world's emptiest and least hospitable places. Greenland's 60,000 citizens have more water than anyone else. Each of them could consume 8 million gallons of it every day if they chose. But having no crops to irrigate or industries to sustain, they need little. In contrast, people in the driest countries have by far the greatest need—to irrigate crops as well as to quench their thirst—but by far the least supply. Ask the Palestinians in their desert enclave of the Gaza Strip. This, the most water-starved political unit on Earth, has just 37 gallons of brackish underground water a day available for each inhabitant, for all a person's needs.

■ Civilizations come and go, but usually water is at their heart. More than 6 millennia ago, the city of Ur was at the center of the greatest civilization on Earth. The people of this metropolis in what is now Iraqi desert ruled over a wide plain between the Rivers Tigris and Euphrates that the Greeks called Mesopotamia. The people of Ur ruled and prospered because it was here that humans first gained mastery over major rivers. The arid plain was transformed by hydraulic works into the granary of the Middle East and was probably the most densely populated area in the world. Today the hydraulic works are gone—and the land is desert once more. The giant ziggurat of Ur was nothing more than a landmark in the sand as U.S. tanks passed north during the Second Gulf War.

It was almost 7,500 years ago when early Sumerians constructed the first known irrigation works on this plain, some 150 miles north of Ur. In the fields they planted the forerunners of modern wheat and barley, which they bred from natural grasses transplanted from the nearby Zagros Mountains, part of modern-day Iran. These early irrigators diverted water from tributaries of the two great rivers in the shadows of the Zagros, usually by digging a hole in the riverbank and channeling water to plots close by. Over the centuries, they moved from the shadow of the hills and spread west across the arid plain into what is now Iraq. They began digging longer canals to distant fields, and in the lower parts of the plain they extended their hydrological mastery by erecting defenses against the floods that poured down the Tigris and Euphrates from Turkey each spring.

Soon the simple farming communities had turned into far larger and more complex social organizations. These, the world's first cities, were ruled at first by all-powerful priesthoods and later by kings and generals. The Sumerians built eight cities, including Ur, Girsu, Umma, and Uruk, each with tens of thousands of inhabitants. Out of the adversity of the desert they created what we now call civilization. As the German hydrologist Gunther Garbrecht put it: "The hydrological chaos of the valleys was transformed into flourishing gardens, fields, and meadows that in mythology were named the Garden of Eden."

In time, other great civilizations sprang up along other fertile valleys across the Old World: most prominently on the Nile in Egypt, the Indus in Pakistan, and the Yellow River in northern China. These extraordinary enterprises were like nothing seen on the planet before. And most remarkably, they all grew up in areas with serious water problems, usually in deserts. Ancient Egypt, a country then as now without significant rainfall, sustained population densities as high as 470 per square mile, a figure double that of modern France. The Pharaohs were able to do this by harnessing the waters of the world's longest river. In the Indus Valley of modern Pakistan, the Harappa civilization flourished in the Sind Desert around its capital, Mohenjo-Daro. It thrived so well on the waters of the great river as it flowed out of the Himalayas, growing such bumper crops of wheat, cotton, and vegetables, that it could set up industrial outposts in India and trade as far as East Africa.

Meanwhile, the valley of the Yellow River was the cradle for a Chinese civilization that became a supreme example of a society dependent on its waterworks. From the time of their arrival on the floodplain 8,000 years ago, Chinese farmers have dug irrigation channels and raised dikes to channel the river's capricious flows. Controlling the river has always been a symbol of good government. The Chinese have a word for it: *shin*, which means both "to regulate water" and "to rule."

Other early civilizations in less arid regions also grew around vast waterworks. In Southeast Asia, the remarkable Hindu and Buddhist empires of Angkor in the jungles of Cambodia constructed canals and dikes and reservoirs to irrigate rice terraces. They controlled the flows of tributaries of the giant Mekong, whose monsoon floods spread across the forest floor each summer—a system that Pol Pot unsuccessfully attempted to re-create during his "killing fields" reign of terror in the country in the 1980s. Early Sri Lankan societies were founded on a network of reservoirs more complex than anything attempted in that country in modern times. Their kings had reputations as irrigation engineers rather than as military men; they were conquerors of nature. The island is today dominated by huge reservoirs and long-distance canals built a thousand years ago by King Parakramabahu to irrigate hillside terraces and river valley fields. Take a cursory look at any modern map of Sri Lanka. It will show a country pockmarked with man-made lakes. The large ones are ancient, the small ones modern.

In Mexico and Peru, the most organized societies and most densely populated areas—often more densely populated than today—were arranged around huge hydrological enterprises. In Europe, the city of Cordoba was the jewel of Moorish Spain, where irrigation water was essential to survival. The city was probably the first in the world to exceed a million inhabitants. That was at a time when London, the largest city in northern Europe and a place where water was easily available from the year-round flows of the River Thames, had a mere 35,000 people.

Throughout most of human history, adversity has been a spur for the social organizations needed to master the elements. And mastery of water, as the most vital and capricious element, was the supreme spur. Karl Wittfogel, an American history professor writing in the 1950s, called these early societies organized around the need to manage water "hydraulic civilizations." He proposed that their complex urban structures and social organizations—with the development of specialized crafts and skills, the sciences, and religious hierarchies—had been born out of the necessity to marshal farmers and coerce slaves into digging and maintaining dikes and canals, and operating sluices and watching for floods. Their societies depended on such organization, but they were also born of it.

Whether in flat desert plains such as those in Mesopotamia; or mountainous country such as Sri Lanka, the Himalayas, or the eastern Mediterranean; or floodplains like the Mekong, the management of water to irrigate crops was the central, defining technology. "Artificial irrigation by canals and waterworks were the basis of Oriental agriculture. Water control necessitated the centralizing power of government," Wittfogel said. "Until the industrial revolution, the majority of human beings lived within the orbit of hydraulic civilizations." The citizens of hydraulic civilizations, Wittfogel argued, were the first to look at the world in a more scientific way, becoming astronomers and mathematicians and accountants as well as hydraulic engineers. The whole edifice of modern urban society, in short, arose out of mankind's desire to control rivers.

Many have criticized Wittfogel's ideas. Exceptions can certainly be found. Although ancient Egypt grew from control of the Nile, there was little need for, or evidence of, central organization. It wasn't necessary. But the idea of hydraulic civilizations retains a persuasive power. On the plains of Mesopotamia, the citizens of the first hydraulic civilizations fought the first water wars over their irrigated fields, orchards, and palm groves. Their records reveal that around 4,500 years ago, the King of Umma sent soldiers to raid fields of his downstream neighbor at Girsu, cutting the banks and spilling water across the plain. The King of Girsu saved his kingdom by digging a new canal to the Tigris. Soon his control of the Tigris gave him a large empire that eclipsed Umma. Tablets dating from this period record that most of Sumer "was watering its fields in joy under him."

Modern societies are more complex. Mastery of water is not enough. Water priests and irrigation engineers seldom rule. But the politics of mastering water across the American West was central to the making of the region, particularly to its brightest star, the state of California. Water, they say, rather than the gun, made the West. And, as China begins work on its south-north diversion and others consider copying it, many believe water will be the twenty-first century's most critical resource—the "new oil"—and that a new breed of hydraulic civilizations, able to organize water management on an unprecedented scale, is about to come to the fore.

■   Whether or not these predictions are right, we are already dramatically altering the Earth's water cycle, with consequences that we are only beginning to comprehend. Some of the world's mightiest rivers no longer reach the sea for much of the year. The Nile courses out of the Mountains of the Moon in East Africa, recharges in Lake Victoria, and traverses the Sahara Desert through Sudan and Egypt via the High Aswan Dam before yielding up the last of its water just short of its natural destination in the Mediterranean. Even in the monsoon season, every last drop is usually taken by the time the Nile wearily meanders through its delta. The Yellow River in China, having watered the cities and fields of half a billion people, is a trickle by the time it encounters sandbars at its mouth and, most years, gives up. The Indus in Pakistan, the Euphrates in Iraq, the Rio Grande on the border of the United States and Mexico, the ancient and once-mighty Oxus in Central Asia—all appear on maps as running to the sea. But maps are one thing; the truth is often different.

Even the rivers that reach the sea more or less intact are suffering indignities along the way that often make them more unwieldy, more prone to flooding and to periods of low flow, or less fecund for fish. Human efforts to tame the floods have often proved misguided. The Mississippi seems to flood more the higher its levees are raised. From the Columbia to the Volga, salmon and sturgeon expire because they cannot traverse dams to reach their upstream spawning grounds. By draining the lakes in the lower Yangtze Valley, China has created floods rather than protected against them. When the river is in spate, the water has nowhere to go.

The death and crippling of these rivers is as damaging for the planet as the loss of our rain forests. But just as the world is becoming increasingly aware of the value of the rain forests in protecting plants, securing people's livelihoods, and stabilizing the planet's climate, so are we coming to realize that the natural cycles of great rivers are also essential for maintaining both the planetary water cycle and human society. And that realization is starting to have practical effects. China may be pushing ahead with its giant Three Gorges Dam and beginning work on its south-north diversion, both larger versions of technologies developed in the United States. But back in the United States, the first home of the great superdams, the government is now tearing down the concrete and freeing water to revive wetlands and fisheries. As Bangladesh plans huge embankments in a final effort to tame the Ganges and prevent its floods, in Europe, home of Dutch dike-builders and German river-straighteners, the governments are breaching the dikes, putting back the meanders, and giving rivers back their floodplains, in the name of ecology and for more reliable protection against floods.

■   As the rivers fail to provide all the water we demand, our assault has turned to underground water stored in porous rocks. The volume of water in these rocks, which geologists call aquifers, is impressive. At any one time there is far more water underground than in all the rivers and lakes on the planet's surface. The Ogallala Aquifer, which stretches beneath six states in the high plains of the United States, helped the region get over the horrors of the Dust Bowl in the 1930s. It contains more water than Lake Huron.

Some aquifers are regularly replenished as rains percolate through soils or incontinent rivers leak through their gravelly beds. But others—including most of the largest—are repositories of ancient and largely immobile water from wetter times. The Ogallala gets some recharge, but only at about a third of the rate at which the water is being pumped out. As a result, the aquifer is already seriously depleted and, at the current rate of pumping (13 million gallons a minute), will be entirely empty within 140 years, though the cost of extracting water from the deepest parts of the aquifer would become prohibitive well before that. What then for the Dust Bowl states, which currently have about a fifth of all the irrigated farmland in the United States? At current rainfall rates, it would take 2,000 years for the Ogallala Aquifer to refill.

The world's largest underground freshwater store is, oddly enough, beneath the Sahara Desert. There lie the remains of water that filtered underground from the huge marshland—a world of bulrushes and crocodile-infested lagoons—that occupied the region until around 5,000 years ago. Then the rains for some reason suddenly and permanently failed, and the Sahara turned within a few decades into the world's largest desert. The average age of the water beneath the Sahara is some 20,000 years, and some may have been there for as much as a million years. Take that water away—as Libya is currently attempting to do through one of the world's largest water engineering schemes, known as the Great Man-Made River Project—and it will not be replaced.

Northern China is draining its aquifers to make up for the diminishing flow of the Yellow River at the surface. As the ground dries, lakes and springs have dried up, once-lush grasslands have turned into dust bowls— and the poorer farmers with the shallowest wells and weakest pumps are left without water. But as the river empties, the rate of recharge also declines—a good reminder that rivers and underground water reserves are intimately connected. There is some rain here to replace the loss, but some 25 million acre-feet more water is pumped out of the aquifer than nature can make good on.

Emptying is not the only threat to aquifers. They are also much more vulnerable to pollution even than the lakes and rivers on the Earth's surface. A single drum of dry-cleaning fluid poured into a hillside could, after a decade or so of percolating through rock pores, dangerously contaminate as much water as it takes to keep every British domestic water tap full for 10 days. Some 40 percent of Kuwait's huge water reserves beneath the desert were polluted by Saddam Hussein when he set fire to the oil wells at the surface during the Gulf War of 1991, and they are now permanently unfit for drinking. Of course, rivers can get contaminated, too. But they flush themselves clean. Aquifers can't.

Aquifers are also physical structures, honeycombs of pore space that can collapse if they are emptied of water. That causes subsidence on the surface, with cracked buildings and highways. But there are other effects, on the aquifers themselves. Overpumping of the aquifers in the Central Valley of California is thought to have destroyed pore space for storing water equivalent to the reservoir behind the Grand Coulee Dam.

■ The good news is that we rarely destroy water. We may pollute it, irrigate crops with it, or flush it down our toilets; but somewhere, sometime, it will return, purged and fresh as you like, in the rain clouds over India or Africa or the American Midwest or the chalk hills of England. Water is the ultimate renewable resource. But with every one of us requiring a hundred times our own weight in water to irrigate the food we grow in a day, the real need is to ensure that water is always where we need it, when we need it—for all 6 billion of us. One approach to doing that is to reengineer the planet's hydrology, as the Chinese are now attempting to do. Such efforts carry price tags in the many billions of dollars, and as resources become ever more remote and difficult to tap, the price will only increase.

History has a way of humbling the grandest human ambitions, and it offers an interesting insight on this point. What, after all, became of those most organized of the hydraulic civilizations of the ancient Middle East? Hunt around the ziggurat of Ur and you find, well, desert. There is an empty landscape with no water, no fields, no soil, and no people. What went wrong? The answer to this puzzle is a much more ancient barbarism than anything inflicted by Saddam Hussein. The irrigation works that made this region finally destroyed it. Tiny quantities of salt brought down by the rivers from the mountains of Turkey and Iran gradually accumulated in the irrigated soils. Archaeologists have traced how rising salinity gradually forced the Sumerians to abandon wheat for the more salt-tolerant barley before even that failed. And as salt overwhelmed the fertility of their fields, the Sumerians abandoned the land and moved north. By the nineteenth century, when Europeans began to visit Iraq, the country had a population less than a tenth of that at the peak of its hydraulic civilizations.

A similar chronology is found buried in the remains of the ancient Harappa civilization in the sands of the Indus Valley, where a buildup of salt caused the soils and crops to fail around 4,000 years ago. More recently, the Angkor civilizations in Cambodia finally failed because the kings allowed the giant reservoirs, known as *barays*, to silt up, and man-made rivers that took water to the reservoirs eroded their beds until their flows were too low to refill the reservoirs.

Given the apparent urgency of our current water needs, do we nonetheless have any choice but to revive the glory days of the hydraulic civilizations? Perhaps here too history offers a lesson. Less heroically visible amid the archaeological remains of the world, there is another, parallel tradition that seems to give greater staying power than the hydraulic civilizations. The world's first town was not, after all, in Mesopotamia or China or Egypt. It was, it seems, on the west bank of the River Jordan. Jericho, 9,000 years ago, was modest enough, nothing like the great cities of Mesopotamia 3 millennia later. It covered just 10 acres and had a thick defensive wall. Inside were a few hundred people and a tower, now the world's oldest surviving man-made structure. And close by was a spring, known in the Bible as Elisha's Spring, that irrigated ancient crops. Today, the spring still gushes 20 gallons a second into ancient irrigation furrows and ditches that distribute its water to the fields and orchards of this desert oasis. The ancient town was destroyed by floods around 8,000 years ago. But the irrigation works live on long after all the Sumerian works have crumbled.

Among the central questions we will explore in the pages that follow is this: to which tradition will we cling as we confront the water crisis currently unfolding around the world? That of the hydraulic civilizations, or that of Elisha's Spring?

PART II

Replumbing the Planet

CHAPTER THREE

Egypt's Source
of Everlasting Prosperity?

No dam excites so much controversy as the High Aswan Dam on the River Nile. It has become the touchstone in the controversy surrounding the philosophy of solving large water problems with large dams and megawater engineering projects. Its supporters say the High Aswan has brought prosperity to Egypt and saved the country from the famines that engulfed its neighbors in the 1970s and 1980s. Its opponents see in its barricading of the Nile, the world's longest river, everything that is wrong with large dams. As the leading American geographer Gilbert White put it, the High Aswan "is both praised as the mainstay of the Egyptian economy and vilified as an environmental catastrophe." Mahmoud Abu Zeid, Egypt's current water resources and irrigation minister and one of the world's leading advocates of large dams, spoke sarcastically when he said that as soon as the High Aswan was completed it became "the most popular environmental problem in the world—a global symbol of environmental and social problems caused by large-scale development projects."

The controversy is so intense partly from history and partly because the stakes are so high. Egypt, after all, is genuinely vulnerable to the fickle flows of the Nile. The Greek geographer Herodotus 2,000 years ago called

Egypt "the gift of the Nile," because without the river's waters it would not exist. The longest-lasting civilization in the world grew up on the banks of the Nile because of the reliability of its waters. Egypt is virtually rainless and utterly dependent on the Nile waters, whose floods in centuries past it diverted onto its fields to grow barley and wheat. On these waters Egyptian civilization has persisted for 7,000 years. Yet, on rare occasions, the floods racing out of eastern and central Africa have failed. The result? In ancient times, dynasties failed. The fear of this failure has fueled a deep historical drive on the part of Egypt's rulers to control the Nile.

The High Aswan for the first time gave Egypt total mastery over the flow in the lower reaches of the River Nile; it is a mastery that offers great potential, but that the dam's critics say is precipitating a long-term environmental disaster for the country's other great resource, the Nile Delta.

The controversy has an extra twist because of the potent political symbolism that surrounded the dam's construction at the height of the Cold War, part of which centered on a battle for control in Africa, and the continuing political tensions caused by the dam's absolutely central role in the politics of East Africa. Those tensions were summarized in the warnings of Boutros Boutros-Ghali, who was foreign minister in Egypt before becoming secretary-general of the United Nations in the 1990s, and who famously declared that the next war in the region would be fought over the Nile. Here's why.

The High Aswan Dam was the brainchild of revolutionary Egyptian leader Gamal Abdel Nasser, who came to power in Cairo in a coup against King Faruk in 1952. He wanted to build an emphatic symbol of his mastery of his country and of Egypt's independence. A dam at Aswan, suggested to him by Italian engineers, seemed the perfect symbol, giving him control over the country's lifeblood, the River Nile. He sought funding first from the World Bank, then a new body just starting out on an era of dam building. But the Americans and the British refused to go along with the plan and vetoed World Bank involvement. Their opposition was partly political. They had supported Faruk and didn't like Nasser. But the U.S. and British veto was also born partly of technical considerations. The British in particular had always thought Nasser's proposed dam site a poor one because the searing desert close to the Sudan border would result in too much water being lost to evaporation. Their engineers had long wanted instead to capture the Nile's waters in the mountains far upstream, as part of a grand strategy for developing the whole region.

But Nasser could not countenance the idea of being dependent for his water on dams in Kenya, or Sudan or Ethiopia or Uganda. He wanted a dam in Egypt. He responded angrily to the West's refusal to back his plan. In 1956, he took over the Suez Canal, which crossed Egyptian land and was then the most important and profitable waterway in the world, announcing that "the canal will pay for the dam." Despite an abortive war by the colonial powers to seize back the canal, that is what happened. And two years later, the Soviet Union, eyeing the chance for a foothold in Africa, stepped in with technical assistance, turning the High Aswan Dam, at least in Western eyes, into a totem of the Cold War.

In May 1964, Soviet engineers began building the huge dam across the bed of the world's longest river. Nasser said of the dam and the lake behind it, which would bear his name: "Here are joined the political, social, national, and military battles of the Egyptian people, welded together like the gigantic mass of rock that has blocked the course of the ancient Nile." It would be "a source of everlasting prosperity" for Egypt. This was grand symbolism for a grand piece of engineering. The dam was nearly 3 miles wide and rose to over 330 feet high. Its volume was seventeen times greater than that of the Great Pyramid. Behind the dam, the pent-up waters created the second-largest artificial reservoir in the world. It wound upstream for 350 miles and widened to 40 miles in places. It could store the equivalent of almost 2 years' flow of the Nile.

The project, which eventually cost about $1.5 billion, would allow farmers to irrigate their land even during the region's persistent droughts. And it would provide Egypt's rapidly expanding population with cheap power and a constant supply of water. Within 4 years, it delivered its first power to the national grid from giant turbines capable of generating more than 2,000 megawatts of hydroelectricity.

Nasser also saw the dam as cementing his country's regional domination. Before building the dam, he had to secure a deal with Sudan, Egypt's southern neighbor, part of which would be flooded by Lake Nasser. The resulting Nile Agreement, signed in 1959, gave Egypt two-thirds of the river's designated annual average flow of 68 million acre-feet; the rest went to Sudan. But Nasser left out of the deal the seven other Nile nations farther upstream: Ethiopia, Uganda, Congo, Tanzania, Kenya, Rwanda, and Burundi. (There is now an eighth: Eritrea.) Instead, he warned them that he would go to war with any that took "Egypt's water."

Of these upstream neighbors, the most aggrieved was Ethiopia, whose territory includes the headwaters of the Blue Nile and the smaller tributaries Atbara and Sobat, which together make up 85 percent of the main river's flow. The White Nile, which arises in Burundi and passes through Lake Victoria before traversing Sudan and converging with the Blue Nile at Khartoum, accounts for the remainder. After the Soviet Union's diplomatic coup at Aswan, the United States retaliated by drawing up plans for four giant dams on the Blue Nile in Ethiopia. None got very far, however. Ethiopia soon came under the control of a Marxist, Haile Mariam

Mengistu, who ruled with increasing tyranny and inefficiency until the end of the 1980s. With Sudan also in chaos, this left Egypt, for the time being, with virtually uncontested control of the Nile's flow through the Aswan High Dam.

■   For its proponents, like Abu Zeid, the argument for the virtue of the High Aswan Dam is simple. Though the dam is not the first dam on the Nile, it was the first to capture the whole annual flood, which surges down the river each September. Total mastery means that river flows downstream of the dam can be kept higher throughout the long dry season. Much of the Nile's long valley and delta can thus be double- or even triple-cropped, often with water-hungry but lucrative cash crops such as rice and cotton. As a bonus, electricity with an annual value of around half a billion dollars is currently generated from the dam's turbines. Farm output in Egypt increased by between 10 and 20 percent within 5 years of the dam's completion, and in the early 1970s the dam's turbines provided half of Egypt's electricity.

The huge storage capacity of Lake Nasser is especially valuable because low-flow years on the Nile come in clusters. There were seven such years in the 1980s. While people starved near the source of the Blue Nile, in part because they were unable to draw significant quantities of water from the river, downstream the High Aswan collected what flow there was and protected Egyptian agriculture from collapse. Egypt did come within weeks of running out of water as the Ethiopian drought reached its climax, but the country, and the reputation of its dam, were saved when heavy rains in the Ethiopian highlands replenished the reservoir. "Water security has been the major contribution of the High Dam to the Egyptian economy," says Tony Allan, a specialist on Middle East water at the School of Oriental and African Studies in London.

But there is another side to this story. The huge dam flooded a very large area of land that was, despite many claims to the contrary, far from being empty desert. At the time when Lake Nasser was filling, most international attention centered on the threatened inundation of great archaeological monuments in the Nile Valley, such as the temples of Abu Simbel. These were eventually moved at great expense, with the aid of an international appeal set up by the United Nations Educational, Scientific and Cultural Organization (UNESCO). But the biggest immediate losers from the dam, about whom much less has been heard, were the 130,000 Nubians, half in Egypt and half in Sudan. They also had to move from their land in the flooded zone. Most ended up impoverished, living in government-built villages of concrete blocks far from the river.

Some of the claims about other impacts of the dam remain contentious. There are debates, for instance, about the reasons for the disappearance from the eastern Mediterranean of the sardines that once bred in the Nile estuaries. Most likely the loss of freshwater flows from the Nile into the sea triggered their demise, but nobody can be sure. The dam is also blamed for the buildup of algae in the river water and the spread of bilharzia, a debilitating disease harbored by the snails that proliferate in the static waters of reservoirs and irrigation canals. But the most serious criticisms, especially when it comes to the long-term consequences of the dam, concern silt and salt.

First, silt. Each year, the Nile brings down around 130 million tons of silt in its muddy flood. Most of this soil came from the Ethiopian highlands. For thousands of years, Ethiopia's loss has been Egypt's gain. Before the dam, around 90 percent of the river's annual load of silt was washed into the Mediterranean. But between 10 and 15 million tons of it was deposited onto the Nile floodplain in annual layers. It kept fields along the

Nile fertile for thousands of years, while other ancient hydraulic civilizations in Mesopotamia and the Indus Valley failed.

Since 1964, however, little silt has bypassed the dam. Instead it is accumulating in layers of about a yard a year on the bed of Lake Nasser. It may be hundreds of years before the buildup of silt seriously reduces the capacity of the huge reservoir. But the dam's critics say the loss of rich soil has already done irreparable damage to the fertility of the Nile Valley and its delta. As a direct result, they say, Egypt is now among the world's heaviest users of chemical fertilizers, and fertilizer factories are among the biggest users of the High Aswan's hydroelectric power. Meanwhile, say the critics, many trace elements once brought to fields in the silt are also in increasingly short supply in the soils of modern Egypt.

Abu Zeid dismisses this analysis. Trace elements have always been in short supply, he says. And Egyptian research shows that Nile silt only ever provided farms with "insignificant" amounts of natural fertilizer. He says that farmers use more fertilizers today because they are growing more crops, not to compensate for lost silt. Whatever the truth in this long-running and contentious debate, there is no doubt that the loss of silt has created other problems. Egyptian brick makers once simply cut their raw material from the riverbanks, knowing that the river would replace it in the next flood. But since 1964 they have had to buy up more and more land to stay in business. This is no small matter. According to White, around 250 square miles of riverbank were eaten up in this way before the government called a halt in 1985 and forced brick makers to move into the desert.

More fundamental is the crisis facing the Nile Delta. The delta contains two-thirds of Egypt's farmland and is a resource of at least equal importance to Egypt as the Nile's water. But in geological terms, it is a rather new and fragile geographical feature. It began to form only around 8,000 years ago, when the stabilization of the sea level of the Mediterranean allowed silt from the Nile to accumulate at the river's mouth. Since then, the delta's fields have probably been cultivated continuously for longer than any others on Earth. But this accumulation ceased almost 100 years ago, when colonial engineers from Europe first built small dams in the delta to divert the river's flow onto fields. That reduced silt flow to the outer edges of the delta. Waves from the Mediterranean began to erode the delta, which stopped growing and began retreating.

At first the retreat was slow, but since the construction of the High Aswan virtually ended all supply of silt to the delta, the retreat has become much more rapid. Much of the delta coastline is retreating by around 30 feet a year, and in places the figure is 800 feet. Fifty years ago, the village of Borg-el-Borellos lay at the mouth of one of the main channels through the delta. Now the village is submerged and more than a mile out at sea. The Nile sediments that reached the sea were once washed eastward along the coast. They maintained the sandbars that sat in front of the delta's large lagoons, protecting them from invasion by the sea. Now the bars are eroding, and their collapse will flood more low-lying delta farmland.

To add to the problems caused by silt starvation in the delta, there is the prospect of a renewed rise in sea level under the influence of global warming. The fear is growing that the delta could be approaching a catastrophe. It would be a brutal irony if the High Aswan Dam, which gave Egypt total control of the Nile, in the process triggered the destruction of the river's delta. But that is now a very real risk.

The second great threat to the delta from the dam is salt. The Nile may no longer bring silt to fields, but it does bring salt dissolved in its water. The modern irrigation systems allowed by the management of the Nile leave the salt behind—approaching half a ton per acre every year. Salt is toxic to most crops. Yields on a tenth of the delta's fields are already being reduced by the salt. Egypt has spent about $2 billion, much of it in loans from the World Bank, on installing a drainage network to remove the salt. The total bill has now exceeded the original cost of the dam itself, and work is far from completed. But there is no choice. If the accumulation of salt is allowed to continue, the fields will become toxic to plants, and the salt could eventually form a crust that would turn them back to desert.

■   If Egypt loses farmland to salt desert in some places, it is determined to use the waters of the Nile to annex more farmland from the desert elsewhere. Successive Egyptian leaders have attempted to create large areas of "new lands" through irrigation. The dream has often proved an expensive nightmare. During the 1960s, Egypt built roads and canals, power lines, and water pumping stations on more than 900,000 acres of desert west of the Nile Delta. Nasser's propagandists named it the Liberation Province. But the coarse, sandy soils of the desert soon became waterlogged. By the end of the 1970s, only a third of those fields were still producing crops. "Unviable projects have been sustained as national fantasies," says Tony Allan, a stern critic of the schemes to create the new lands.

Undeterred by such failures, Egypt is now planning another assault on the desert. It wants to irrigate a further 1.5 million acres in the Western Desert by siphoning off water from Lake Nasser and storing it in new lakes, to be known as the Toshka Lakes. Echoing the boasts of his predecessors, President Hosni Mubarak calls this "the project for the millennium." The lakes are set to become the center for a new agricultural and industrial region in the desert. The first farm was bought by a Saudi prince, indicating where Egypt anticipates much of the money for the $5 billion 20-year project will come from.

The project will eventually need some 4 million acre-feet of water a year to thrive. It got off to a good start when, during bumper rains in 2000, Egypt was able to divert a total of around 25 million acre-feet out of Lake Nasser, over a spillway, and into the lakes. That's fine, perhaps, in a good year. But what happens if there is a succession of bad years, like those in the 1980s? Even Abu Zeid has admitted in the past that if these desert schemes go ahead, Egypt could face serious water shortages in the future. He has calculated that the country's annual water deficit will exceed 11 million acre-feet by the year 2025.

To forestall such shortages, Egypt wants to perform the seemingly impossible and increase the flow of the Nile. Its target is the As Sudd, a vast and remote area of wetland on the White Nile in southern Sudan. The waters of the White Nile spend a year or more meandering through the As Sudd before they come north. During that time, roughly half the flow of the White Nile is lost to evaporation in the searing heat and near-permanent sunshine. If the time the water spends in the As Sudd could be shortened, then more water would make it through to the High Aswan Dam.

The original idea of digging a canal to bypass the As Sudd and reduce the evaporation losses is credited to William Garstin, a British engineer who was head of public works in Egypt a century ago. But it was 1978 before engineers got down to work. They brought to the shores of the As Sudd an extraordinary giant Rube Goldberg device that they called a "bucketwheel," which described it quite well. It was a giant laser-guided wheel as high as a five-story house, to which were attached huge buckets designed to cut a channel through the desert. Funded jointly by Egypt and Sudan, the Jonglei Canal was planned to reduce evaporation from the White Nile by 4 million acre-feet a year. This water was to be divided equally between the two nations.

However, the early 1980s were not a good time to dig a canal through the badlands of southern Sudan. The region was in turmoil as the Muslim north of the country tried to impose its will on the non-Muslim south. Religious ferment was compounded by a realization in the south that Khartoum was more interested in digging the canal to fill taps in Khartoum and Cairo than it was in providing clean drinking water for the villages of the Dinka herdsmen along the canal route. Worse, the bucket-wheel's vast trench would carve right through Dinka pastures and prevent them from taking their cattle into the As Sudd swamplands during the dry season. It probably didn't help when, in his effort to sell the project to the locals, Sudanese vice president Abel Alier chose a herding metaphor to announce that "if we have to drive our people to paradise with sticks, we will do so for their own good and the good of those who come after us."

On February 10, 1984, the newly formed Sudan People's Liberation Army (SPLA) attacked the bucketwheel camp. Its guerillas destroyed everything except the great machine itself and, in a gun battle with government troops, killed an Australian pilot and hightailed it with some hostages, who were eventually released unharmed a year later. The French engineers abandoned their bucketwheel. It remains to this day in the desert beside its half-dug canal. $100 million spent for nothing.

This was no ignorant assault on water engineers going about their lawful work. There was serious purpose in the choice of target. The head of the SPLA, then as now, was one John Garang, a member of the Dinka tribe but also a Sudanese beneficiary of an American education in the 1970s. He has a doctorate in agricultural economics from Iowa State University. More than that, he wrote his doctoral thesis on the damaging environmental consequences of the Jonglei Canal Project. In it he argued that the canal would suck southern Sudan dry of its greatest resource—the waters of the As Sudd. After his education, he returned as an army officer to Khartoum before defecting to join his fellow Dinka tribesmen in rebellion and to head the new movement. Twenty years on, there is fitful peace in southern Sudan. During peace talks in 2003, Garang hinted that, if the terms were right, he might eventually allow construction of the Jonglei Canal. Betrayal or pragmatism? We shall see.

■   There is more bad news for Egypt from the Nile's headwaters. The 1959 agreement between Egypt and Sudan to carve up the waters of the Nile assumed an average annual flow down the river of 68 million acre-feet a year. But for much of the time since, the river has not lived up to expectations. During the 1980s, the average was 62 million acre-feet. During the drought years between 1984 and 1987, the average fell to 42 million acre-feet. In 1984, the year that John Garang and his rebels ambushed the bucketwheel camp and thwarted the Jonglei Canal construction project, the Nile had its driest year in a century.

Things recovered during the 1990s, encouraging Egypt to embark on the controversial Toshka Lakes Project. But some climate models predict that as global temperatures rise, rainfall in Ethiopia will fall, reducing the flow of the Blue Nile, which provides the majority of the main river's flow. Declan Conway of the Climatic Research Unit at the University of East Anglia calculates that a reduction in rainfall of 10 percent in the Blue Nile catchment will cut runoff into the catchment by 35 percent. Meanwhile higher temperatures will increase evaporation rates still further, especially from Lake Nasser, the As Sudd, and the lakes at the head of the White Nile, losing more precious millions of acre-feet.

Until now, Egypt has been able to maintain the quantity of water it takes from the Nile largely because Sudan does not use its full entitlement under the 1959 treaty. But that could soon change. Egypt's unfettered rule of the Nile's flow through the High Aswan may shortly be over. Despite the turmoil in Sudan, the government in Khartoum is intent on refurbishing its existing derelict dams and building new ones. In 2002, Sudan announced plans to throw some 50,000 Nile Valley dwellers off their land to make room for its own mini-Aswan dam at Merowe, north of Khartoum. It also intends to clean out reservoirs built by British engineers in the 1930s that have since silted up and lost much of their storage capacity. The cleaned-out dams will capture Nile flow for planned new Saudi-funded sugar plantations along the banks of the Nile.

More worrying still for Egypt's water planners is that Ethiopia may soon be making its own demands on the waters of the Blue Nile, drawing on the proposals prepared by the United States a generation ago. Egypt has plans for big new irrigation works and reservoirs with a combined capacity of around 40 million acre-feet, equal to the entire annual flow of the river in some years, and for irrigation works capable of consuming more than 4 million acre-feet of water a year.

In its anxiety to find more water, Egypt is looking again at ways to reduce evaporation from Lake Nasser. The unrelenting Saharan sun draws more than 6 feet of water from the surface of Lake Nasser each year. This is an average total loss, Abu Zeid estimates, of almost 11 million acre-feet, or more than twice the quantity lost from the As Sudd, and enough to meet the entire current water demand of England. The best way of reducing this loss would be to store water away from the desert in cooler places, such as in the headwaters of the Blue Nile, where evaporation rates are a third of those on the arid Nile plain. In hilly terrain, the reservoirs could also be deeper, so a given volume of water stored there would have a smaller surface area, further reducing evaporation.

Garstin knew all this 90 years ago. That is why he recommended the construction of large reservoirs in the headwaters. British hydrologists, who effectively ruled the Nile until the 1950s, backed Garstin's proposals and opposed construction of the Aswan High Dam because they believed that its losses to evaporation would be unacceptably high. Nasser emphatically rejected this advice. But now, with Egypt's hydrological independence fading, the idea is set for a revival.

The unlikely truth is that Egypt's salvation could lie in giant dams being built outside its borders, in Ethiopia. Storing around 40 million acre-feet of Blue Nile water in its headwaters could do much of the job that the High Aswan Dam currently does, while saving millions of acre-feet of water that currently evaporate each year. If Egypt and Ethiopia could agree on how to share out that water, then both could be winners.

Such a grand settlement cannot work if the talk continues to be of "water wars" on the Nile. International rivers such as the Nile may generate tensions, but the invaluable resource they represent can be managed efficiently only if there is stability and cooperation. The remorseless logic of hydrology dictates that water could be an agent for peace as much as for war. The High Aswan Dam did not, as Nasser had hoped, place the future of Egypt in the hands of Egyptians, nor guarantee his country "everlasting prosperity." On the contrary, it seems to have left Egypt more vulnerable than ever to its upstream neighbors.

CHAPTER FOUR

Killing the Nigerian Floodplains

On a riverbank on the desert margins of northern Nigeria, a hundred or more youths, wearing bright pink shorts and wielding a fishing net in each hand, stood poised to plunge into the muddy waters. At a signal they all rushed into what remained of the river at this the midpoint of the long dry season. In a seething mass of flailing nets and bodies, they plunged to the bottom and fought for the fish in the pools of water left behind by the river as it dried up. Northern Nigeria's Gorgoram fishing festival, a celebration of nature's bounty every February on the edge of the Sahara Desert, had begun.

It may have been one of the last. Engineers have been raising dams that will shut off the flow of the rivers that sustain the fish in this particular river, and the lives of the fishermen who depend on it. In a region of Africa better known for drought and famine, the dams are held out as a source of bounty for a parched region, a way to green the desert margins. But they could do the opposite. The natural lakes and floodplains support a million or more people and provide exports of fish and vegetables to cities to the south. If the dams close off the annual floodwaters, as their designers intend, then the lakes will dry up entirely most years, and the floodplains where the fish spawn and feed and grow will cease to flood. In a region with a population density greater than that of California, the desert will take over.

Half an hour after taking to the water, the glistening youths were carrying fish up the steep banks to a huge pair of scales erected in front of a grandstand. Three local emirs and a national presidential candidate watched as the fishermen of Gorgoram weighed the whiskered catfish, still twisting in the midday sun. There were prizes for the best hauls—a bicycle for one team, a mechanical sewing machine for another. But it was clear that the festival, the high spot of the local year, was a shadow of its former self. The scales could accommodate individual fish weighing up to 220 pounds. The largest fish caught that year weighed just 10 pounds. Everyone made the best of it. The prizes were duly awarded. But the youths looked disappointed and resigned. The girls watching the youths looked cheated. There were no heroes that day. The crowd started to drift away, the promise of the river and its fish seemingly forgotten.

As we left, bouncing along the 30 miles of dirt track that winds past one of the emirs' palaces toward the nearest tarred road, there was more evidence that the wetlands here are dying. The landscape was littered with fallen trees—victims of a sinking water table. Behind us, clouds of dust rose on the desert wind. This is the story of an African disaster in the making. It is not, for the moment, a disaster that makes headlines. There are no starving children, no airlifts of grain, no refugee camps, no visits from aging rock stars. But I may have been looking at the start of a silent, stealthy ecological apocalypse that a decade or so from now will grab the world's attention. By then it will be too late to help.

■ The Hadejia-Nguru Wetland, of which Gorgoram is a part, is a bulwark against the desert. It is a kite-shaped oasis stretching for more than 75 miles along the Hadejia and Jama'are Rivers and their numerous mean-dering branches on the edge of the Sahara, east of Nigeria's great north-ern city of Kano. There are permanent large lakes here, through which herds of cattle wade, grazing on the lush grasses. The lakes are a popular wintering ground for European birds, too. Around the lakes are wide areas of fertile soils that flood seasonally, known in the local Hausa language as *fadamas*. The rivers flood the fadamas each summer, allowing fish to breed in profusion and wetting the soils so that farmers can plant rice as the waters recede. Sometimes there is enough moisture left after the first crop is harvested to plant a crop of cowpeas in the dry season as well. And everywhere the floods recharge the underground waters that nourish woodlands and keep the region's simple hand-dug wells full in even the driest years.

In a region where virtually all the rain falls in August and September, the wetlands are a vital resource. And the annual river flood is the driving force behind almost every aspect of the local economy. Yet for almost 30 years, successive Nigerian governments and their Western advisers have sought to "develop" these desert margins by undermining the ebb and flow of the flood—to capture water that they considered wasted if it ever entered the wetlands. They have tried to green the dry land by catching the water behind dams and diverting it to large irrigation projects. But far from greening the desert, their efforts seem set to turn the wetlands into a dust bowl.

The first large dam here, the Tiga Dam, was built in 1974. It diverted a tributary of the Hadejia River to feed a state irrigation project south of Kano. Now, each wet season, the rain that falls on the hills above the Tiga Dam must replenish the reservoir and supply the irrigation project before the sluices are opened and any spare flow is allowed onto the wetlands. The

situation has deteriorated further with the completion of the Challawa
Gorge Dam. Since the completion of these two projects, the amount of
land regularly flooded in the wetlands has fallen by two-thirds to less than
400 square miles.

As I traveled through the wetlands and the surrounding farmland, both
the farmers and the nomadic Fulani herdsmen who pass this way each
year bemoaned the loss of their waters. Women near the market town of
Nguru gossiped and flirted as they hauled water in leather pouches from
a concrete well dug by the government just 2 years before to replace
another that had run dry. But the men said: "The water is no good for
farming here anymore. It doesn't flood so well these days." At the lakeside
village of Likori, a farmer rested on his hoe as he pointed to a deeply
cracked field—an old fadama that used to be watered by the flood. Without regular floods, his crops will no longer grow there. On Punjama Lake,
out in the middle of the wetland, boys pushed their way across the water,
belly-down on calabash gourds, paying out hundreds of yards of fishing
line. Less water meant there were fewer fish, they said. Wheat and vegetable farmers who irrigated their fields by pumping water out of the river
using small Yamaha pumps said there was often no water to pump. Their
crops were dying in the fields.

In the weekly market at Gashua, the easternmost town on the wetland,
fish were in short supply. Instead, the market was filled with bags of
potash, the salty crust of the desert soils scraped by villagers from shriv-
eling oases to the north. Outside Gashua, I drove past a camel train bearing yet more potash for the market. It had just crossed a dried-up branch
of the River Yobe. Once this was one of the main rivers draining the wetlands, but it went dry soon after the Tiga Dam closed its sluices and has
never come back. Today the riverbed that stretches through near-desert

close to the border with neighboring Niger is nothing more that a sand-filled depression. Camels walk where fishermen once threw their nets.

Across the wetlands, surface waters have disappeared since the Tiga Dam was built. The water table has also fallen by 80 feet in places, and wells have dried up for hundreds of miles. It is difficult, of course, to distinguish between the effects of the dams and those of the droughts that have ravaged the region in the past three decades. But even in moderately wet years, when the rainfall is as good as it was back in the 1960s, the old lakes do not refill. Calculations by hydrologists suggest that the Tiga Dam and its adjuncts are responsible for at least half of the wetland's decline. Only during exceptionally wet years like 2001, when the dam managers are intent on releasing water to save their structures from inundation, does the full flow of the rivers reach the wetland. And then it usually happens in an unnatural rush, with little or no warning. In 2001, emergency release resulted in a tidal surge across the wetland unlike anything that a natural flood would have produced. Instead of fecundity, it brought destruction, leaving behind 200 inundated villages and a hundred dead.

This is just the start. More dams are planned. The Challawa Gorge Dam was built to supply the Hadejia Valley Project, a vast French-built irrigation scheme under construction on the edge of the wetland. And still to come is the Kafin Zaki Dam, a structure on the Jama'are River that was left half completed after the money ran out. If it is ever finished, it will be the largest dam of them all. The whole of northeastern Nigeria—the stretch of desert margin running for 400 miles from Kano to Lake Chad—appears on the brink of hydrological disaster. As one expatriate British water engineer living in Kano told me: "We are living on the hydrological edge. We have seen in Ethiopia and Somalia what happens when the water runs out.

We could soon have a similar situation here. And if it happens the disaster will have been man-made."

The boys floating across the Punjama Lake on their calabash gourds didn't know it, but their lake and its fish could soon disappear altogether. And conflicts over what remains of the wetlands loom. As the sun began to set, a white orb in a desert haze stirred up by the harmattan wind, the boys headed for home. They disturbed flocks of pintail geese and storks that flew across the glistening water. And they called to a Fulani herdsman. He too was wading slowly for home as his cattle munched through grasses in the waist-high water. They asked him to keep his cattle clear of their fishing lines.

Once there was room for all. Fishermen could keep clear of cattle, and farmers were happy to let the herdsmen onto their land during the fallow season. But not now. Farmers and fishermen, the permanent residents of the wetland, vie for the resources with migrant cattle-rearing Fulani, who depend on the wetlands to graze their animals during the dry season. Months before my visit, there had been a pitched battle between the two groups on the wetland near Gorgoram. Ten Fulani had died. Three years before, they had collected the dead at Kissingen fadama after herdsmen organized an invasion of old pastures that had been fenced off by farmers. In Kano, a social scientist told me: "Serious disputes only began after the Tiga Dam was built. Now almost every fadama has seen battles over water and grazing rights. Every year, people get killed."

■ Nigeria is often called the China of Africa. One in every five Africans is a Nigerian. Since the 1970s, the government has decreed that large dams feeding great irrigation projects will make the country self-sufficient in food. But so far these efforts have produced a catalog of social, economic, and environmental disasters. In northwestern Nigeria, at Bakolori on the Sokoto River, farmers occupied a dam construction site after being expelled from their land to make way for an irrigation project. The police moved in, and after the shooting and burning died down, 386 farmers lay dead. The project has since halved the natural flooding in the valley, and fish stocks have declined. Some fishermen left for good and ended up on the Hadejia Wetland. Now the engineers, and the conflicts, are following them there.

So what have been the economic benefits of all this engineering and all this environmental destruction on the wetland? The Tiga Dam was built to provide water for the Kano River irrigation project—an American idea, funded by the British and finally built by the Dutch. When finished 20 years ago, it had cost $40,000 an acre to construct, making it one of the most expensive irrigation schemes ever completed in Africa. Yet ever since its completion, crop yields on its fields have been around half those anticipated. Only a third of the rents due from farmers are ever collected. It is a financial millstone for all concerned.

When I visited the project, most of the fields were empty. I counted a dozen individual farmers' plots before I found anyone at work. I walked down miles of irrigation canals, all full of water evaporating in the midday sun, but saw only two farmers removing water for their fields. I met a consultant from an international irrigation institute commissioned by the Nigerian government to find out what had gone wrong. She threw her hands in the air. "The Hausa are just lazy," she told me. "They sleep under the trees all day. There's nobody in the fields when I want to ask them questions." She was right that the fields were empty. But the Hausa had their reasons, and laziness wasn't really the story. Many fields were waterlogged because the field channels had been dug at too shallow a gradient and had filled with silt and thick mats of grass. The waterlogging was bringing toxic salts to the soils and made it impossible to grow wheat, the most profitable crop. Most farmers had other jobs and treated their expensively irrigated fields as little more than weekend allotments. Poorer farmers were selling their land.

There could not have been a greater contrast with fields on the natural wetlands downstream. There, crowds of farmworkers were bent double hour after hour, clearing soil with small hand hoes, ready to plant beans in the wet soil as the lake waters retreated. These fields, though much diminished in extent because of the dams, cost nothing to irrigate. Nature did it for free. And looks do not deceive. Hydrologists calculate that every acre of field irrigated by the Kano project dries out more than 2 acres of wetland. Yes, they found, the Kano irrigation project produces more food for every acre of land than does the wetland. In that narrow sense, you might call it a success. But in northern Nigeria, the critical resource is not land, but water. And while, according to a recent economic study of the situation by Ed Barbier, an environmental economist at the University of Wyoming, every acre-foot of water delivered to the Kano River Project produces an economic return of just 5 cents, a similar amount reaching the wetland produces an economic return of $1.50 from farming, fishing, and timber.

That amount was leaving out less easily quantified benefits, such as the meat, milk, and hides from livestock; the honey from beekeeping in the wetland woodlands; the mats, baskets, and rope made from the leaves of local doum palm trees; the bricks dug from muddy pools and baked dry in the sun. These could easily double the wetland's economic value, said Barbier. And even this does not account for the ecological value of the wetlands to the thousands of migrating birds stopping over here on their route to Europe, or the wetland's role in recharging the region's wells. It amounts to economic insanity to destroy such natural fecundity.

■ I traveled on east, downstream of Hadejia on the road to Lake Chad and the border with Niger. Everywhere I found ominous hints of the future awaiting the wetland. Maiduguri, the largest town in northeastern Nigeria, has exhausted two aquifers and now pumps underground water from a third, a hundred feet beneath the surface. But with dams like the Tiga and Challawa Gorge holding back flooding from local rivers, that aquifer too is emptying. The town will die unless a new source of water can be found, say exasperated European aid officials.

Past Maiduguri, at Kirenawe, stands one of the outstanding monuments to the folly of big irrigation projects in Africa. The South Chad Irrigation Project is a British-built multimillion-dollar scheme intended to use water from Lake Chad to irrigate fields of cotton and rice and wheat. Its purpose was to green the desert. But it is high and dry, miles from the nearest water, and its fields have sat useless for almost 3 decades as a lethal combination of Sahelian drought and diversions by dams has sent Lake Chad into full-scale retreat. During the dry season, the lake's shores are some 40 miles away from the project's water intakes. Indeed, the shoreline is in another country, over the border in Chad. The irrigation project's canals and pumping houses, its intake works, and the grain mills built to take its produce stand abandoned.

The Tiga Dam, the Challawa Gorge Dam—and maybe soon the Kafin Zaki Dam—have ostensibly all been designed to green the desert. But in practice they are stealing water from people who know how to use it and giving it to those who do not. In so doing, they have created a permanent, man-made drought and have given the Sahara Desert another victory in its march south. Development, anyone?

CHAPTER FIVE

A New Force of Nature

Perhaps the greatest threat to dams and to those who live downstream of them comes not from flooding rivers but from earthquakes. A disturbing number of dams actually cause earthquakes because the weight of water in their reservoirs disturbs the local geology and triggers small shifts along fault lines. As many as a quarter of the world's superdams have triggered some earth tremors as their reservoirs filled. This can happen even in areas with no history of earthquakes. Normally the tremors are small. But not always. The filling of a reservoir at Koyna, near Bombay, in 1967 seems to have led to a shock of magnitude 6.5 on the Richter scale in a region of otherwise low seismicity. It broke the dam and killed 177 people. The dam was rebuilt after the disaster, but in late 2000 it emerged that the new dam also had cracks in it, caused by more recent tremors.

The big fear is that a large dam, with hundreds of thousands of people living downstream, will be hit by a major natural earthquake. A large number of dams around the world are sited close to geological faults or in regions known to be seismically active. Occasionally there are disasters, as when the Machu Dam in the Indian state of Gujarat collapsed in 1979 during a quake, drowning an estimated 2,000 people in the town of Morvi.

Sooner or later, something bigger seems certain to happen. Nobody can make firm predictions, but a likely candidate is India's Tehri Dam, being built today on the headwaters of the Ganges, in a seismic zone and close to the site of a recent earthquake.

■   There are new occupants in the palace of the old maharajas of Tehri Garhwal, high above the town of Tehri in the western Himalayas. They are engineers from the Tehri Hydro Development Corporation, and they have designs on the valley. They plan to drown it by building here the tallest dam in South Asia. And you can see why. Tehri is a wonderful place for an engineer to build a dam. It is the narrowest point in a narrow Himalayan gorge at the end of a wide, trough-shaped valley that will soon hold almost 3 million acre-feet of water. Indian geologists picked out this valley 30 years ago as a prospective dam site. And in the 1990s they began work on a dam 850 feet high, close to Tehri town, where two tributaries of the River Ganges join. Behind it, the Bhagirathi Valley will be flooded for 30 miles and the Bhillinganga Valley for almost 25 miles.

In the plains south of the Himalayas, the citizens of New Delhi want more water for their taps, and the industrialists of cities like Kanpur and Allahabad want more hydroelectricity for their factories. Farmers right across northern India, the country's breadbasket, are desperate for the dam to provide both water for the irrigation canals and electricity to help to pump yet more water from underground to irrigate their fields. The people expelled from Tehri, however, are less enthusiastic about the $2 billion project. Even as the earthmovers were completing the dam around them in late 2003, they were holding daily protests through the ghost town that most have now been forced to evacuate.

As this book goes to press, the first power is expected to be generated from the Tehri Dam's turbines in early 2005. The reservoir will flood Tehri town and twenty-three villages in the valley, displacing more than 80,000 people. But the 300,000 inhabitants of three towns downstream—Haridwar, Devaprayag, and Rishikesh, home of the Maharishi Mahesh Yogi—would also be well advised to move out when the dam is completed, for seismologists believe there is a serious risk of a large earthquake in the valley within the lifetime of the dam. And they fear that if the expected quake strikes, there is a real risk that it could destroy the dam and send the contents of its reservoir surging down the rapids through the narrow gorge into the towns below.

Shivaji Rao, head of the college of environmental engineering at Andhra University and a government adviser on dams, has this bleak prognosis for the Tehri Dam: "If the Tehri Reservoir emptied in half an hour, floods would reach Rishikesh in one hour and Haridwar in another 15 minutes. A 130-foot wall of water would rush down the narrow valley. Almost all the people in Devaprayag, Rishikesh, and Haridwar may be killed, and all towns and villages up to Meerut, some 150 miles from Tehri, may be severely damaged."

In 1993, with work well under way on the project, there was a quake just 30 miles from the dam site. Hundreds died as buildings collapsed on them. In the aftermath, seismologists from around the world called for a halt to the Tehri Dam's construction. But the dam's engineers successfully resisted the call, and work continued. Jim Brune, a former president of the Seismological Society of America and a professor of geophysics at the University of Nevada, was one of those who called for a halt. He says the Tehri Dam is "one of the most hazardous in the world from an earthquake point of view."

The epicenter of the 1993 quake was, he says, in the middle of a "seismic gap" that extends for 500 miles through the Himalayas along the boundary between two continental plates. A seismic gap is a zone along a plate boundary where stress is building up because of an absence of large earthquakes in the recent past. The gap runs between Kashmir in northwest India, scene of a quake measuring 8.6 on the Richter scale in 1905, and Bihar in the northeast, where an 8.4 quake struck in 1934. The 1993 quake measured 6.4. Since the Richter scale is logarithmic, the 1993 quake was a hundred times smaller than the other two. It was far too small to relieve the strain along the gap. "The stress is still being stored up for the big one, which could come at any time. There is a clear possibility of a quake with a magnitude greater than 8," says Brune.

However, according to Brune, in the arcane and competitive world of seismology, "the engineers who are advising the Indian government do not believe in the idea of seismic gaps." Brune, like most working seismologists, does. And he calculates that "although we cannot predict precisely the time of the future quake, there is little doubt that it will occur sometime in the next few hundred years and has a high probability of occurring during the projected lifetime of the dam."

■ Could the 850-foot-high dam stand the impact of such an earthquake? Brune thinks there is a real risk that it would not. Indian engineers seem to have juggled the figures to pretend otherwise. This is what happened.

Although the main fault line through the area has experienced quakes of 8.6 in the past, the Tehri Dam was originally designed to withstand a quake of only magnitude 7.2. This was on the advice of engineers from the University of Roorkee in India, who first investigated the area for the Indian government. The engineers calculated that such a quake could move the ground at the surface with an acceleration as great as 0.446 g

(g is the acceleration due to Earth's gravity). So the dam was designed to resist an acceleration of 0.5 g.

However, in the early 1990s, seismologists such as Brune began to express concern that this was not enough. The Indian government commissioned a report from a new committee of experts, mostly engineers. The new committee accepted the advice of its lone seismologist that the dam should be able to withstand a quake of at least 8.0 on the Richter scale. But the engineers then revised their estimate of what that larger quake might mean for ground acceleration. They concluded that even an 8.0 quake would not achieve peak ground acceleration of greater than 0.446 g. So, presto, the original dam design was good enough after all.

Brune, the man who first devised the formula for calculating peak ground acceleration from earthquakes, says this was foolhardy. And worse, the committee has misused his formula. The formula was derived for calculating quakes in the soft rocks of California, he says, and cannot be directly applied to a hard-rock mountainous region like the Himalayas, where the force of a quake could be amplified through the hard hills rather than being muffled by soft rocks of the kind found in California. "There is extreme danger not only from the major fault, but also from numerous branching faults which might rupture the crust much nearer the dam than the main fault itself," he says. Like water rushing into a narrow valley, branching faults can concentrate the force of an earthquake, producing even greater "ground acceleration" than the rupture of the main thrust, says Brune.

"There is no question that accelerations greater than 1 g might be produced at Tehri Dam. The question is, What is the probability, and what risk is acceptable? In my opinion this question deserves much more investigation," says Brune.

And, he warns, even a quake too small to destroy the dam on its own could cause large landslides around the edge of its reservoir. These would trigger huge waves of water that could themselves destroy the dam. Such an event happened at the Vaiont Dam in the mountainous region of northeastern Italy in 1963, killing 2,000 people. Again, Tehri seems a prime candidate for disaster. Thirty years ago, the Geological Survey of India noted in an early project report for the Tehri Dam the remains of "a number of major landslides along the River Bhagirathi. These slides are expected to be aggravated during conditions of rapid drawdown of the reservoir," it said, and predicted "a few more fresh slides" near the dam itself. Since then, the dam has been earmarked as a source principally of "peak load" electricity for the state grid in Uttar Pradesh. This means that the dam's turbines will be switched on and off frequently, alternately raising and lowering the water levels in the reservoir—giving precisely the "rapid drawdown" identified by the geologists as dangerous.

Finally, there is the risk of a reservoir-induced earthquake. When the Tehri Reservoir fills, its water will weigh 3.5 billion tons. Harsh Gupta, former director of India's Centre of Earth Studies and vice-chancellor of the Cochin University of Science and Technology, says that the fractured and crushed rocks of the Bhagirathi Valley will increase the risk of a reservoir-induced earthquake. The broken rocks, he says, will allow the weight of the reservoir above to force water down into zones where it could trigger earthquakes. Tehri is a disaster waiting to happen.

■ There are today some 800,000 dams around the world. Some 45,000 of them are more than 50 feet high; more than a hundred tower 500 feet or higher above the rivers they are intended to tame. If all the water in all the reservoirs behind all the dams in the world were collected together, it would measure 8 billion acre-feet. It would cover half of California to a height of 130 feet. If it were all released into the oceans, it would raise the sea level on every beach around the world by some 8 inches.

Of the 45,000 large dams more than 50 feet high, almost half are in China. Another quarter are divided between the United States and India, followed at a distance by Japan, Spain, and Canada, with Turkey and Brazil fast catching up to them. Their construction was one of the great engineering enterprises of the second half of the twentieth century. Since 1900, the world has on average completed one large dam every day. Their turbines generate a fifth of the world's electricity, and their waters irrigate a sixth of the world's crops. They barricade 61 percent of the world's river flows.

These dams have even changed the shape and rotation of planet Earth. The water in their reservoirs is so heavy that it deforms the Earth's crust and unleashes periodic earthquakes. And by shifting water away from the equator, where ocean water is concentrated, they have altered the speed of the Earth's rotation in much the same way as ice skaters speed up by pulling their arms in close to the body. The "reservoir effect" has so far shortened the length of the day by about a thousandth of a second. The asymmetrical distribution of reservoirs around the Earth has even tilted the Earth's axis. The North and South Poles and every line of latitude and longitude are now 2 feet from where they would otherwise have been.

Dams are more than an earth-shaping technology. They have great power as totems of modernism and as symbols of a very mechanistic notion of how mankind can "tame nature." Rivers, in the modern vision created in considerable part by the engineers at the U.S. Bureau of Reclamations (BuRec), are no longer fickle, tempestuous, meandering, flooding, fish-nurturing, floodplain-invading, silt-bearing, canyon-cutting forces of nature. They are channels of water to be tamed and corralled by concrete.

And that perception has swept away all recognition of older, more environmentally benign and sustainable—indeed, arguably much more sophisticated—technologies for managing water.

Although most of the early large dams were built in the United States and the Soviet Union, they swiftly became emblems of modernization in the developing world. In the United States, following the dam-based economic development of the Tennessee Valley Authority, they also became symbols of the New Deal and of progressive politics. Dams offered the prospect of unlimited renewable energy. Woody Guthrie sang an anthem to the virtues of the Grand Coulee Dam as "the greatest wonder in Uncle Sam's fair land."

They have been the biggest callers on international aid budgets for the past 50 years. Every developing nation wants its Hoover Dam. Independent India's first prime minister, Jawaharlal Nehru, a convinced modernist and industrializer as well as the heir to Mahatma Gandhi, called his dams "the new temples of India." Egypt's High Aswan Dam—built by Russian engineers at the height of the Cold War—captured the annual flood of the Nile. Ghana's Akosombo Dam flooded an area the size of Lebanon, evicted 80,000 farmers, and virtually bankrupted the nation in the process.

Dams are promoted as serving a variety of vital roles, all of which seem to be in increasing demand around the world. They provide protection against floods at a time when floods are responsible for 40 percent of all deaths from natural disasters. They provide water for cities and industry at a time when more than a billion people lack access to clean drinking water. They deliver much of the irrigation water that has fed the green revolution of the past 40 years, more than doubling world food production and keeping pace with population growth. And they generate electricity without burning fossil fuels. Switzerland, Austria, Sweden, Brazil, and Norway all use dams to generate more than half their electricity.

The United States may be tearing down its dams, but in the fast-expanding economies of Asia in particular, the era of dam building, especially to generate power, is still in full swing. Big is still seen by many as beautiful. China's newest and biggest, the Three Gorges Dam, would if transplanted to Europe generate enough electricity to power the Netherlands. China is now also building a string of huge dams down the headwaters of the River Mekong. Malaysia is flooding the rain forests of Borneo to power its industrial revolution. India continues to build dams as fast as it can. Electricity is Laos's biggest export. Nepal and Bhutan, two small nations sitting astride the Himalayas, the "water tower of the world," want to exploit the huge amounts of water in seasonally melting glaciers to become the sheiks of hydroelectricity.

CHAPTER SIX

Libya's Great Man-Made River

It is one of the largest tracts of true desert in the world. The 700 miles from the coast of Libya inland to the oasis of al-Kufra and beyond into Chad, northern Sudan, and western Egypt are so bereft of water holes and vegetation that even camel trains didn't cross the Libyan Desert until the nineteenth century. But beneath the endless sands lies one of the largest masses of freshwater on the planet. The Nubian sandstone aquifer dates back to the last ice age, when the Sahara was a vast swamp from which water constantly seeped into the sandstones that formed a layer several miles thick on the African bedrock. The aquifer carried on filling until probably around 6,000 years ago, when the region abruptly switched from a land of marshes and crocodile-infested rivers to the desert of today. Since then, give or take a little infiltration from flash floods in the Tibesti Mountains to the south, the aquifer has sat unaltered. Though all trace of past climate has gone from the surface, its legacy remains intact underground.

Drill down into the desert, and after about 1,600 feet you tap water. Keep drilling and the water keeps coming. Saturating the pores within the sandstone rock, this reservoir is as deep as the ocean. There is an estimated 120 billion acre-feet of water down there. That is enough to cover the desert to a depth of about 250 feet, or to keep all the world's taps and irrigation canals flowing for about 30 years. At the bottom, more than 2 miles below the surface, the water may be millions of years old.

And drill down is what Libya has done. Thanks to one of the least known but largest engineering projects ever undertaken on the planet, Colonel Muammar al-Qaddafi has for the past decade been pumping upwards of 400 acre-feet of water a day out of this giant aquifer and bringing it by pipeline all the way to the populated Mediterranean coast—to where the aquifers that once provided irrigation water for the country's date orchards and grain farmers have been emptied by overpumping and invaded by salty water from the sea.

Qaddafi opened his first pipeline one hot desert night in the summer of 1991. Watched by a throng of African leaders, he compared his great work to the pyramids of ancient Egypt. A thousand Libyans rushed forward to take ecstatic sips of a precious liquid that had lain untapped in the pores of the Sahara's subterranean sands for many times longer than the pyramids have graced the desert.

The pipeline into the desert is Libya's one and only "river"—Qaddafi calls it his "Great Man-Made River." But rather than the water emerging spontaneously from a natural spring, it has first to be pumped up some 1,600 feet from a thousand boreholes sunk into oasis regions such as al-Kufra. The water takes 9 days traveling to the coast down a metal pipe that is big enough to drive a tank through—a fact leading to some stories a few years ago that the pipe was really a cover for Libya to invade its neighbors. Qaddafi is still extending his Great Man-Made River, with a second pipeline in the west of the country and an eventual linking pipe that will allow the entire country to be supplied with Nubian sandstone water at a rate of perhaps 5,000 acre-feet a day. When fully operational, the great artificial rivers will pump each day a volume of water equal to half the volume of oil that gushes from all the world's oil wells.

■ The well is one of the earliest and most universal sources of water. Many communities across Africa and South Asia still lift water in buckets by hand or use animals driving treadmills. Until the second half of the twentieth century, the great majority of wells relied on gravity and muscle power—which placed effective limits on the amount of water that could be lifted and from what depth. But just as the large dam transformed our ability to harness the water from rivers, so cheap drilling rigs and diesel and electric pumps on sale in tens of thousands of stores around the world have given tens of millions of poor farmers the means to extract unprecedented amounts of water from beneath their fields. Meanwhile, the wide availability of cheap, subsidized electricity for pumping in many countries has meant that they have been able to carry on doing so as water tables plunge hundreds of feet below the surface.

But this level of extraction cannot go on. The aquifers will eventually determine the limits to which farmers can go. The danger is that the limit will increasingly be when the water runs out. To see poor Indian farmers leaving their pumps on for 24 hours a day to remove water from up to a mile beneath the ground to water their rice and wheat crops is to understand that this is a finite resource under grave threat. Even as geologists are learning for the first time how to map and quantify the great reservoirs of water beneath the ground, many of these same reservoirs are being destroyed.

Despite the billions of dollars being spent on dams, and on canals to channel water from the dams to fields, small farmers in many countries increasingly rely on water pumped from beneath their fields. Even when surface water is available from state irrigation projects, farmers will often choose to pump their own water because they have greater control over when they get water and how they use it. In large parts of the world, particularly the arid areas where surface water is running out, underground supplies are now a bigger source of water than rivers. Many of the world's largest cities also now depend not on the rivers beside which they were formed but on underground water, much of it brought long distances. These cities include Bangkok and Beijing, Cairo and Calcutta, Manila and Mexico City, Shanghai and Tehran, Lima and Dhaka.

In Iran, 50 percent of water comes from beneath the ground; in India and in Syria, the figure is 60 percent; in Bangladesh, 70 percent; and in Saudi Arabia, more than 90 percent. Between them, India, Bangladesh, Pakistan, China, and Nepal use more than 240 million acre-feet of underground water a year—nearly half the world's total annual use. In India alone, 120 million acre-feet are extracted.

Being out of sight, underground waters are often taken for granted. But in many parts of the world we are now mining water on a vast scale. Underground water reserves, sometimes containing water tens of thousands of years old, are being emptied far faster than nature can refill them. The aquifer beneath northern China, one of the world's largest, is being overdrawn at a rate of 25 million acre-feet a year. In places, the water table is falling by 20 feet a year. In parts of Gujarat and other states of western India, whole villages are being abandoned as the wells run dry. In Iran, a third of the grain harvest is irrigated with underground water that will not be replaced by the rains. In Saudi Arabia and Yemen, Mexico and Pakistan, there are similar stories.

Some experts nonetheless see groundwater as the world's great untapped water resource. As fast as farmers drain the aquifers, scientists are discovering new ones and enlarging their estimates of the capacities of others. The newly mapped Guarani Aquifer stretches beneath four South American countries: Brazil, Argentina, Uruguay, and Paraguay. It may soon supply water to São Paulo, the world's third-largest megacity. There are still large reserves in several more of the world's largest aquifers, such as the Nubian sandstone aquifer beneath the Sahara and Australia's Great Artesian Basin.

■   Is this a sign of the future? A future in which humanity will stop moving to where the water is and instead will bring the water to its own front door? Or is the sound of water down Qaddafi's $25 billion pipe the death rattle for the kind of Stalinist engineering hubris that insists on remaking the world in iron and concrete? For despite all the hyperbole, Qaddafi's river is, in hydrological terms, quite modest. Even if all five phases are completed, they will irrigate fields that could comfortably be fitted twice over into Delaware. That works out at some $10,000 worth of water supply infrastructure for every acre of irrigated land, making those fields among the most expensively watered fields in the world.

    And the water will not flow forever—even assuming Qaddafi's engineers can plug the leaks and repair the corrosion that, according to persistent reports from the secretive state, seemed to be afflicting the pipe only a decade after it opened. For while Qaddafi talks of "several hundred years of potential production," his engineers admit that within perhaps 50 years his pumps will have lowered the water table near the wells by 300 feet or more. It will then become prohibitively expensive to carry on, even under Qaddafi's fantasy economics.

■   Some say no water reserve should be emptied faster than nature can refill it. We should not mine our water reserves. Others ask, why not? If we can take oil, then why not water? That is Colonel Qaddafi's view. He believes the Nubian Aquifer can do for his farmers what the Nile and the Aswan Dam have done for Egyptian farmers. And Qaddafi's strategy is catching on. So-called fossil waters, which many believe should be kept back as strategic water reserves for use only in an emergency, are increasingly being seen as suitable for day-to-day use. In the parched conditions of the Middle East, the Qaddafi approach is gaining ground, not least because Qaddafi is offering his expertise to help other countries mine their nonrenewable water sources on a scale that makes other potential funders cringe.

Take Jordan, a country suffering greater water stress than almost any other. The Jordanian capital, Amman, has since the 1970s been deprived of most of the flow of the River Jordan by an upstream diversion in Israel. Thus it has relied increasingly on pumping dry an oasis 70 miles away in the country's eastern desert. But the pumping out of the Azraq Oasis has had its inevitable consequence. The springs that sustained the oasis, a world-famous haven for wildlife, have begun to give out, and some years the vegetation becomes so dry that fires break out across the oasis. Despite recent efforts to replenish the Azraq Oasis by pumping water from a nearby aquifer, it is clear that a permanent new source of water is required for the Jordanian capital. Jordan now plans to tap another fossil aquifer, beneath the Disi Basin in the far south of the country, at a cost in pipelines and pumps of around $700 million. On a goodwill visit to Amman in 2000, Qaddafi promised to send spare pipes left over from the Great Man-Made River Project to make the 200-mile link from Disi to Amman.

How much water will Disi provide? How fast should it be tapped? Here, as with Qaddafi's domestic projects, things get murky. Reports from the United Nations University (UNU), which has been monitoring the plans for the project, said at the start that Disi is Jordan's "last substantial unexploited water resource" and should be kept "for emergency use only." Some chance. The Disi Aquifer is already being tapped for the nearby town of Aqaba as well as by local farmers. So, accepting political reality, the UNU proposed instead that output should be capped at 14,000 acre-feet a year, with the pumps running for a maximum of 50 years. By that time, it said, an alternative source of water for Amman should have been developed and what remained of the Disi Aquifer could be put back into cold storage.

But the numbers keep going up. The United States Agency for International Development (USAID), which is reluctant to see Jordanian water fall under Libyan influence, now suggests that a whopping 40,000 acre-feet could be taken out annually for 100 years. But even that is not enough for Jordan and its Libyan partners. Thanks to the giant pipes to be imported from Tripoli, the Jordanian water minister, Hatem al-Halwani, was able to report in 2003 that he planned to draw more than 80,000 acre-feet of water annually to fill taps both in Amman and in a wide area of southern Jordan. The Disi Aquifer seems to be lined up for extinction.

CHAPTER SEVEN

A Second Front in the Green Revolution

In India, more than 60 percent of the country's irrigation water now comes from underground. That is double the proportion from as recently as the late 1980s. More than 20 million Indian farmers pump water from beneath their land, often from depths of hundreds of feet. An extra million farmers join them each year in a rush to tap the retreating waters before they disappear altogether. As state irrigation projects fed by large dams falter, many farmers say they have little alternative. One estimate is that Indian farmers have invested $12 billion in pumps in the past 20 years. And even farmers with access to state irrigation water like the flexibility that their own water sources gives them.

Indian farmers extract an estimated 210 million acre-feet of water from beneath their fields each year. That may be twice the rate at which the water is replaced by the monsoon rains. It is a free-for-all in which nobody is capable of managing who does what or who takes what. In places, water that could be hauled from the ground using a rope and bucket 30 years ago now requires electrical pumps working day and night to bring it from up to half a mile below the surface.

One potential constraint on pumping is the price of fuel. But with politicians handing out huge subsidies to small farmers for electricity, that is a constraint of little consequence. Until 2003, Punjab, one of the breadbasket states of northern India, provided free electricity to its farmers. More typically, farmers across India's northern breadbasket pay around $10 a month to be allowed to run one or more 7.5-horsepower pumps for as long as the power system will supply electricity.

In reality, the only limit on pumping is the capacity of the country's electricity generating system. Widespread blackouts are being caused by farmers' attempts to pump day and night. When the power fails, they are forced to stop pumping—though many will persist by switching to diesel-powered pumps, or even hooking up their tractor engines to power the pumps.

But in this resource anarchy, the water is giving out. Water tables are plunging across some of the most productive areas of agriculture in India. Tushaar Shah, a leading expert from the International Water Management Institute, based in the Indian state of Gujarat, says: "Fifty years ago in northern Gujarat, bullocks driving leather buckets could lift water from open wells sunk to about 30 feet. Now tube wells are sunk to 1,300 feet but still run dry." In the southern state of Tamil Nadu, I met farmers pumping 24 hours a day from an aquifer in which the first water appeared a mile down. Every few weeks, their wells went dry, and they brought in commercial borehole drillers to go down farther. But still the pumping continued. Many farmers have become so hooked on the process that rather than growing crops, they were selling the water, either to other farmers or to city industrialists.

Surely, say many Indian politicians, the only answer is to replumb the nation to take the water from its big northern rivers to where the people are. Under the BJP government, which lost power in mid-2004, the president and prime minister, most state governments, and the Supreme Court—agencies that in India's complex democratic system spend much of their time in internecine warfare—united to promote what is known here as the River Interlinking Project. Only by tapping the country's great northern rivers, they believe, can India continue to feed itself. India's National Water Development Agency in New Delhi, which is also backing the scheme, says there will be enough water to irrigate some 80 million extra acres of farmland—an increase of more than 50 percent—and to power 34,000 megawatts of hydroelectric capacity, although as much as a third of this could be needed for pumping water around the scheme's network of canals and tunnels.

■ During 2003, as China embarked on its south-north project, Indian politicians lined up to back plans for the River Interlinking Project. It will redraw the hydrological map of India, building dozens of large dams and hundreds of miles of canals to link fourteen rivers that drain the Himalayas in the country's wet north. These include the subcontinent's two biggest rivers, the Ganges and the Brahmaputra, both swollen by monsoon rains and the melting glaciers of the Himalayas. And then the project will pump the waters of these rivers south along a thousand miles of canals, aqueducts, and tunnels to fill a second network, comprising the seventeen major rivers of the country's arid south, including the Godavari, the Krishna, and the Cauvery.

India's desire to circulate water around its vast and sometimes parched country is understandable. Thirty years ago, the world was gripped by the specter of mass starvation. Billions, we feared, would die as the world's population doubled in a generation. And India stood closest to the brink. A succession of famines suggested that some kind of Armageddon was approaching. Then came the green revolution. Scientists defied the doom-sayers by breeding new supercrops that kept the granaries full. And in the process, India, whose population has doubled, nonetheless went from being a basket case forever on the verge of famine to a country that exports rice most years. But India, like most green revolution countries, did it as much through the application of water as through the use of new seeds. Green revolution crops were designed by crop breeders to guzzle water and turn it into greater volumes of grain.

With India's population predicted to increase by 50 percent within the next half century, overtaking China to reach a staggering 1.5 billion people, demand for water to feed everyone can only rise. But meanwhile the water is running out.

Today the world (and India) grows twice as much food but uses three times more water. That is why India's rivers are running dry, and why its politicians see a drive to find more water for the parched regions as a national priority.

But many of the people who guided the green revolution believe that the drive to provide water by redistributing it round the country is doomed. For one thing, there is not enough water. For another, there is the economics. The volume of water to be moved in the scheme India now envisions will be similar to China's scheme. But the price tag will be two to three times higher, with official estimates of between $112 and $200 billion, or around 40 percent of the country's current gross domestic product.

■ For another, the scheme risks major confrontations. The project will flood an estimated 2 million acres of land and leave some 3 million people homeless. There could be water wars between Indian states over who gets the water coursing through the national hydrogrid. Already there have been deaths during riots between farmers in Karnataka and Tamil Nadu, two drought-prone southern Indian states fighting over the waters of the Cauvery River. Each state has dams on the river and large canal irrigation systems that depend on them. And each claims prior rights to access part of the flow of the river. For more than a decade, there has not been enough flow to go around. Inevitably, the upstream state, Karnataka, is in the driver's seat, resolutely refusing each year to deliver downstream the water that Tamil Nadu expects and demands. When the politics reach fever pitch, usually during a drought, the conflict generally spills over into riots. In 1992, twenty-five water rioters died in Bangalore. A decade later, after the worst drought in the state for 40 years, India's Supreme Court ruled that Karnataka must release water downstream. Farmers blocked the state's main highway to protest against the releases. The government responded by shutting schools and colleges and suspending all train services. The state virtually shut down as thousands of riot police broke up demonstrations with teargas and surrounded the main dams to prevent angry farmers from invading them. And farmers in the villages of Uttar Pradesh in northern India, who have seen their own wells empty through excessive water use, told me they would take violent action to protest any efforts to take "their" water south.

The river-linking project also seems certain to provoke an international confrontation with Bangladesh, which gets much of its water from the Ganges and Brahmaputra as the rivers leave India. India and Bangladesh have been at loggerheads over water since 1974. That was the year in which India completed the Farakka barrage on the Ganges close to the border. India used the barrage to divert the Ganges' last waters into Indian irrigation canals during the final weeks before the monsoon, when water supplies are at their shortest. Today, thanks to the Indian diversions, the Ganges barely reaches its own delta in Bangladesh during the dry season. Bangladesh blames the Farakka barrage for dried-up fields, disease, and the salt poisoning of the vast Sundarban mangrove swamps on its coastline. Under a 1996 treaty between the two countries, India promised not to reduce flows across the border any further. But now it is planning to do precisely that. In late 2003, Bangladesh water minister Goutam Chakrawarty announced: "We'll launch huge protests; we'll go to the international community, international financial institutions, and the international media to make India abandon its River Interlinking Project, which could spell disaster for Bangladesh."

India's agricultural miracle, which has taken the country from the verge of famine to an exporter of food, could be coming to a crashing end. A quarter of the country's food production is threatened. States such as Gujarat, Tamil Nadu, Punjab, and Haryana are on a knife-edge. Half the wells across western India are now out of commission because the water has failed. Many have been replaced by new wells dug deeper, of course. But whole districts of states like Gujarat are starting to empty of people.

Countries surely have the right to choose what they do with their own water even if outsiders see it as shortsighted. But out in the agricultural heartlands of Asia, in the densely populated plains of India, and elsewhere, something different is happening. Hydrological anarchy is consuming the underground water reserves. And it could very soon have tragic consequences for today's beneficiaries. Shah says that the Indian crisis, though still localized, is destined to spread fast across India and soon across much of Asia. "If left unmanaged, the overuse of water in Asia's underground aquifers will spell disaster for millions of the region's poor people," he says. But quantity is not the only crisis threatening Asia's growing addiction to underground water. . . .

CHAPTER EIGHT

The Devil's Water

Abdul Kasen lifts a green leaf bandage to reveal a large growth on the palm of his hand. It is cancer. Five of his six children also have skin blemishes and cancers. No wonder. They all drink from the same well: a well whose water is laced with arsenic. His well, in the village of Barai Kandi near Dhaka, the capital of Bangladesh, is one of millions across the country that pump up water containing dangerous amounts of the toxic metal, which is a slow poison.

I visited the village in late 1998 with Akhtar Ahmad of the Bangladeshi government's National Institute of Preventive and Social Medicine in Dhaka. Ours was the first visit to this village by anyone equipped to test the water—and we found that all the wells in the village were contaminated. The arsenic coming out of the wells of rural Bangladesh is turning into one of the biggest-ever outbreaks of mass poisoning, and foreign aid agencies are to blame. Water from wells funded and promoted by Western public health engineers over the past 25 years is putting an estimated 30 million people in Bangladesh alone at risk of developing fatal cancers.

Next I went to Chandipur, a typical rice-growing village of 5,000 people in the southeastern district of Laxmipur. This time I was with doctors from the Dhaka Community Hospital, which first raised the alarm about arsenic in the wells of Bangladesh. When the doctors checked 800 people in Chandipur, they found 286 with the early symptoms of arsenic poisoning: skin blotches, keratoses, painful warts that begin on palms and soles and gradually cover the body, acute conjunctivitis, and breathing difficulties. I met Malabar, a 10-year-old boy whose skin was speckled with white blotches, and his friend Kawsar, who was covered in sores and could barely walk. "For these boys the prognosis is dreadful," said Susan Evans, a consultant dermatologist from Liverpool, who was with us and examined 130 villagers in one morning. She diagnosed symptoms of arsenic poisoning in most of them.

A woman, Kulsun, showed the ulcers on the soles of her feet. Another man had sold his land to buy his wife useless medical treatment from a quack. "She used to be the most beautiful girl in the village," he confided quietly. Safiq, an elderly man, pleaded with us: "Please come and test my well to see if the water is safe." But the evidence of his own body, skin blotched and eyes bloodshot and swollen, said that it was not safe. Several patients told us their relatives had died young showing similar symptoms. And Evans confirmed: "These skin conditions are just the outward and early signs. Many of these people will eventually die of internal cancers."

In Chandipur, almost every household has its own simple hand pump for bringing water from the local aquifer for drinking, cooking, and washing. Of 166 wells sampled in Chandipur, the average arsenic concentration was thirty times the World Health Organization (WHO) safety limit. Six of them registered arsenic concentrations at a hundred times the standard. The people in these villages are very vulnerable to any water contamination. Working in the fields in the hot sun, they typically drink 1.3 gallons of water a day. And they consume still more through the water used to boil their rice. Often the rice itself is contaminated with arsenic from the irrigation water.

Chandipur is one village among tens of thousands, each with similar stories. In Samta, in the southwestern district of Jessore, only 5 out of 282 wells are safe. So far, 330 people have arsenic poisoning. I visited other villages where a third of the people had symptoms, and met people with amputated legs, gangrenous toes, and gruesome skin cancers. The World Bank estimates that more than 40,000 villages "are presently or could in the future be at risk."

One of the original discoverers of the epidemic is Dipankar Chakraborti, director of environmental studies at Jadavpur University in Calcutta. He says, "One of the worst villages I have ever visited is Stadium Para in Meherpur District, right on the border with India. Here 9 residents have already died of cancerous ulcers caused by arsenic. One was only 25 years old." But after 5 years of surveying, he nominates the southeastern village of Seladi as "in all probability the most arsenic-contaminated village in the world." Here 72 out of 73 tube wells are contaminated. No fewer than 21 contain arsenic at more than a hundred times the WHO limit, and the highest weighed in at four hundred times the limit.

In some villages, almost everyone is affected. In other villages, only a minority are poisoned. But they may suffer worst of all. "Nobody wants to come in contact with them," says Jinat Nahar Jitu of Dhaka Community Hospital. "They are barred from coming out of their homes or even from using water from clean wells." Wives are divorced and children turned away from schools, primarily out of an unfounded fear that they may infect others. That is what happened to Pinjra Begam, a pretty 15-year-old, shortly after her marriage in 1988 to Masud Rana, a millworker. Her skin became mottled and blotchy. The blotches turned to ugly sores that became

gangrenous. Her husband left her for another. Cancer took hold and spread
to her lungs. She finally died in her home village of Miapur Paschim Para,
near the banks of the River Ganges, aged just 26. She left three children,
ages 7, 5, and 1. Soon Pinjra's children will also likely develop the same
symptoms as the arsenic levels accumulate in their bodies.

■ Arsenic is a slow killer. The most obvious early signs are the blisters
found on the palms of the hands and soles of the feet, which can eventually turn gangrenous and cancerous. Meanwhile, the poison also attacks
organs, notably the lungs and kidneys, which can result in a battery of illnesses, including internal cancers. According to Allan Smith, epidemiol-
ogy professor at the University of California at Berkeley, who has toured
Bangladesh to report on the crisis for WHO, what we see today is just the
beginning. Keratosis, the most unambiguous early symptom of arsenic
poisoning, takes 10 years to develop. With the large numbers of tube wells
dug in the last decade, he says, "a major increase in the number of cases
can be projected." He believes that in much of southern Bangladesh, a
tenth of adult deaths could soon be from arsenic poisoning.

The story of how this happened beggars belief. In the 1970s, international agencies headed by the United Nations Children's Fund (UNICEF)
began pumping millions of dollars of aid money into Bangladesh for the
sinking of wells to provide "clean" drinking water. This was at a time when
most Bangladeshis living in the countryside relied on surface ponds and
rivers for their drinking water. But these surface waters were increasingly
contaminated with sewage bacteria. The country was suffering an epidemic of waterborne diseases, which at the time killed a quarter of a million children each year. So UNICEF sought to solve the problem by insti-

gating a massive project to tap into underground water sources using simple hand pumps attached to bored tube wells.

Villagers were at first wary. Some called this subterranean water "the devil's water." Who knows why? Was there some ancestral memory of past experience? Maybe they were just cautious. Anyhow, they were right. And the Western public health professionals—who were so keen to encourage Bangladeshis to drink the new water that they never checked the water for basic natural poisons—were wrong when they simply assumed that underground water was safe.

In fact, the levels at which most boreholes were sunk by UNICEF and others, at between 60 and 300 feet, coincided exactly with the peak concentrations of arsenic in the water underground. Deeper wells would generally have been safe. So would shallower ones have been. And according to WHO, the direct result of that mistake has been to unleash one of the biggest outbreaks of mass poisoning in history. Up to half the country's tube wells, now estimated to number 10 million, are poisoned. At current progress, finding them all is likely to take decades. Meanwhile, researchers warn that the annual death toll from arsenic poisoning, which is currently 1,000 or so, could eventually reach 20,000 a year.

Even now, as the scale of the calamity emerges, nobody is admitting culpability. Not UNICEF, which initiated the tube wells program and paid for the first 900,000 wells; not the World Bank, a fellow sponsor; not the Bangladeshi government; not the foreign engineers and public health scientists who for so long did not think to test the water. The same agencies that played godmother to the catastrophe are now wringing their hands and saying it will likely take 30 years to find all the poisoned tube wells— longer than it took to sink them all.

UNICEF explains today that "at the time, standard procedures for test-ing the safety of groundwater did not include tests for arsenic, [which] had never before been found in the kind of geological formations that exist in Bangladesh." But many geochemists, such as John McArthur at Univer-sity College London, scoff at such a suggestion. They blame dogma among public health people with no knowledge of geology, who equated under-ground water with safe water.

When government researchers from the British Geological Survey made the first serious tests of the chemical safety of Bangladesh's under-ground water in the early 1990s, they surveyed water from 150 tube wells at different depths, including samples from areas where more than three-quarters of wells used for drinking water are now known to contain lethal concentrations of arsenic. But arsenic was not among the twenty-two parameters that the scientists tested.

That the arsenic remained undetected led to a further delay of 5 years in the uncovering of a public health disaster worse than Chernobyl or Bhopal. Doctors failed to implicate tube wells in unexplained cases of arsenic poisoning that they saw in increasing numbers at local hospitals after 1985, says Quazi Quamruzzaman of the Dhaka Community Hospi-tal. In the end, Bangladesh only discovered the epidemic when doctors compared notes with colleagues over the border in the Indian state of West Bengal, where a smaller outbreak of arsenic poisoning among people switching to tube wells had been spotted by doctors in the mid-1980s. And it wasn't until 1998 that the Bangladesh government finally accepted that it had a problem and the international community agreed to accept some responsibility for solving it.

That year, the World Bank announced an emergency 3-year program to identify the killer tube wells using simple tests and to "put in motion concrete actions [to] combat a major health crisis with devastating effects on the lives of millions." With almost every one of the country's 68,000 villages potentially at risk, the bank said it would initially survey 4,000 villages and draw up action plans for each. This "fast-track project" was to be the first phase in a 15-year program to screen the country's tube wells.

But, even now that the scale of the crisis is understood, this "fast-track" program has proceeded at a snail's pace. It took a whole year for the bank to negotiate with the Bangladeshi government on how to proceed. The bank spent more than a year publicly denying claims by independent experts that the Bangladeshi government had proved incapable of deciding how to spend the money. But it finally emerged in mid-2003—two years after the "fast-track" program should have been completed—that the Bangladeshi government had spent less than $7 million of the $32 million allocated by the bank.

■   There is no way of predicting which of Bangladesh's 10-million-plus tube wells are safe and which carry a promise of disease and death. Neighboring villages, and often even neighboring households, drink water with vastly different levels of poisoning. There is no alternative but to test almost every tube well in the country. It seems likely from surveys so far that water from about half of all the country's tube wells, in more than 40,000 villages, exceeds the WHO limit, many by several hundred times.

In the first step of the mammoth task of testing the country's tube wells, volunteers, aid workers, and officials paint the dangerous ones red, indicating that they should only be used for washing. The villagers are supposed to drink only from the safe wells, painted green. But that is not easy when the only safe pump is in someone else's backyard. (And safe wells may not remain safe. Chakraborti recently reported disturbing new evidence from Faridpur District in India, where some wells tested in 1995 as safe are becoming contaminated.)

In the longer run, part of the answer lies in sinking deeper wells to tap cleaner water. But not every household could have a deep well. It will take thousands of dollars to install each of these wells along with the surface tanks and pipes that would be needed to distribute their waters. Could the tube well waters be treated? While a large number of ideas for filters and chemical treatments have been tried out in the past 5 years, there is "no proven affordable arsenic removal technology available yet," according to Khawaja Minnatullah of the World Bank.

Another idea is to return to traditional methods such as ponds and tanks to harvest rainwater. This will work in some places, says Shahida Azfar from UNICEF, but "there is not enough rain all year for that to be feasible as the main strategy." Some enthusiasts for rainwater harvesting disagree. But without proper trials nobody knows. And there is, of course, a real risk that a return to traditional methods might result in a return to traditional curses, such as fecal bacteria.

Most experts warn against blanket solutions. Each village needs its own plan. And none of them can begin planning until it knows which of its tube wells are pouring poison into villagers' buckets. In his September 2000 report, Smith warned that "the worst thing that can possibly be done is nothing." But for most Bangladeshis caught up in this disaster, nothing is exactly what is being done.

■ Geologists badly need to know where the arsenic comes from, not least so that they can begin predicting if any other parts of the world could be similarly afflicted. In this case, the metal seems to originate in the Himalayan headwaters of the Ganges and Brahmaputra Rivers. Over thousands of years, the rivers dissolved the metal in tiny concentrations and brought it to the great delta of the two rivers, which spreads across most of Bangladesh and West Bengal. There it accumulated in the thick layers of fine alluvial mud smeared across the area by the rivers and has lain largely undisturbed ever since. The arsenic concentration measured in the mud today is not extraordinary. Time is the culprit. The delta mud lies thicker, wider, and flatter than in almost any other river delta system on Earth. It can take hundreds or thousands of years for underground water to percolate through the mud to the sea. All the while it is absorbing arsenic. And if its flow is interrupted by wells and the water brought to the surface, then it is humans who ultimately take it into their bodies.

This slow geological process helps explain the diverse pattern of arsenic concentrations in tube well waters. The contaminated wells almost all take water from a depth of 60 to 300 feet. Shallower wells are clean because they contain mostly recent rainwater or water flowing swiftly through the sediments. Deeper wells tap water in older sediments that have by now been flushed clean of arsenic. It will take thousands of years before the rest of the arsenic will wash away into the Indian Ocean.

Until recently, it was thought that the arsenic was confined to the delta region of these two rivers. But during 2003 it emerged that the epidemic may not be so limited. New studies suggest that arsenic is present in underground waters pumped to the surface all the way up the Ganges Valley as far as the Himalayas, a region occupied in all by some half a billion people. In Bihar, the Indian state immediately upstream of West Bengal, 80 percent of the population drink water from underground sources, mostly using the same type of simple hand-pumped tube wells seen on the delta.

Most of these tube wells in Bihar have never been tested for arsenic. But in 2002, Kuneshwar Ojha, a schoolteacher living close to the river, became concerned after his wife and mother both died of liver cancer and other family members developed skin lesions. He took water samples from the family tube well and sent these to Chakraborti, who found high concentrations of arsenic in them. Subsequent investigations revealed that 18 young people had died from apparently arsenic-related illnesses in the same village in the past 5 years, and a hundred more were sick with early symptoms, such as skin lesions. The only fit people, Chakraborti notes wryly, are the Dalits, or untouchables. Because of their lowly status, they are not allowed to drink water from village tube wells. They still drink dirty surface water.

In the months that followed this discovery, hundreds of similar cases emerged in the same district, and the authorities banned people from using many tube wells. Parts of the original village, Semria Ojha Patti, are now abandoned. By mid-2003, Chakraborti was reporting that a survey of 3,000 tube wells in the region around the village had found that arsenic levels exceed the WHO limit in 40 percent of cases. And 12 contain water at more than twenty times the limit. More than half of adults examined showed symptoms of arsenic poisoning.

"The same pattern we saw in Bangladesh is being repeated," Chakraborti says. "There, we began with the discovery of three villages. Now thousands are known to be affected, and more are being discovered all the time. Our early warnings were ignored then. Now we are warning about Bihar. We feel that this is just the tip of the iceberg."

How big could this get? Also in 2003, doctors in Nepal warned that 10 million people in the Terai Plain, part of the Upper Ganges Valley, may be drinking contaminated water. Many already have symptoms of arsenic poisoning. Chakraborti says that large numbers of the half-billion people living on the Ganges Plain, from crowded northern India to the delta region of Bangladesh, could be at risk. He may be exaggerating, but with few health checks and no tube well studies, nobody knows. One thing known for sure is that because the poison builds up slowly in the body, every year of extra exposure increases the risk.

Is the Ganges Valley alone? It seems unlikely. Though Smith believes that poisoning is probably an order of magnitude greater in Bangladesh than anywhere else in the world, many underground water sources around the world do contain some arsenic. Parts of Taiwan, Argentina, Chile, and China have all suffered epidemics of skin diseases, gangrene, and cancer as a result. Smith's analysis of the Taiwan epidemic in particular helped set the WHO arsenic standards for water and is the basis for his current predictions for Bangladesh.

Another expert, Jack Ng of the University of Queensland in Australia, has found that people are at serious risk in seventeen countries around the world—including China, Argentina, and even the United States, where many communities are failing to meet new arsenic limits set by WHO, albeit not by the same breathtaking dimensions as in South Asia. Vietnam is also facing its own arsenic crisis. Recent tests by Michael Berg at the Swiss Federal Institute for Environmental Science in Dübendorf show that groundwater from tube wells sunk beneath the Red River delta, home to 11 million people, including the capital, Hanoi, contains arsenic levels up to 300 times the WHO safe limit. Symptoms of arsenic poison could soon emerge, says Berg, as people accumulate poisons from tube wells, which were first installed only 7 years ago.

■ Nor is arsenic the only poison afflicting the world's aquifers.

The tiny village of Hirapur in the central Indian state of Madhya Pradesh seemed indistinguishable from millions of others across the world's second most populous nation. But the sight of 10-year-old Shatap changed all that. When I met him one morning in mid-1998, he had a gait straight out of Monty Python's silly walks, except that this diminutive figure was not playing games as he waddled up the muddy lane, his knees locked together and his stunted and misshapen lower legs splayed wide like a seal's flippers. His gait was permanent; his bones were grossly deformed by fluoride in drinking water.

The first rains of the monsoon were beginning to fall as Shatap and his friends assembled outside the home of the head of Hirapur village, Chudaman Bhavre. Almost all of them were knock-kneed and had the brown-stained teeth characteristic of the first stages of fluoride poisoning. They had all drunk water from a poisoned pump while attending the village primary school at the bottom of the lane. Fluoride levels in the pump's water were eleven times the international safety limit. The children who lived nearest to the pump and drank its water continuously had suffered most. Now that the pump has been shut, many of them drink from an ancient open well.

Besides Shatap, there was Kamala and her bowlegged sister Krishna, both daughters of the village head. Age 14, but looking no more than 9, Krishna told me she had been forced to abandon schooling after primary school because her deformed limbs could not carry her to the secondary school in a neighboring village. Many of the parents of these children, including Krishna's mother, suffered painful, stiff, and misshapen backs and hips, and chronic gastroenteritis, as a result of the fluoride. Bhaskar Raman, a local activist who brought the village's plight to the attention of doctors, says there has been an epidemic of stillbirths and involuntary abortions—other known symptoms of fluoride poisoning.

The school pump at Hirapur was installed, like many of the arsenic wells in Bangladesh and eastern India, during the United Nations International Water Decade of the 1980s. The well was one of tens of millions sunk worldwide in a highly publicized race to provide the world's poor with "safe" drinking water, planned and partly funded by aid agencies such as UNICEF. The underground water was indeed mostly free of the bacteria that can infest polluted surface water. But, as in Bangladesh, nobody ever tested the underground water around here for natural chemicals. In Hirapur, that meant they didn't know about the fluoride.

Like many poisons, fluoride is not always harmful. We need it. Small amounts of fluoride help to combat tooth decay. Fluoride attacks the enzymes in the mouth that manufacture the acid on which the bacteria that cause tooth decay feed. This is why water companies sometimes add fluoride to public water supplies. But too much fluoride causes mottled teeth and damages the rest of the body in various ways.

The body absorbs fluoride mainly through the gut. It excretes some through the kidneys and sweat glands, but if we consume too much, the fluoride will gradually accumulate in the body. Fluoride binds strongly with calcium, and so it usually builds up in the same places as calcium, like teeth and bones. That usually doesn't matter too much. But in people with a poor diet that is short of calcium—and that includes most rural Indians—fluoride crystals will often take the place of calcium in their bones. Those crystals increase the density of the bone, putting pressure on nerves and blood vessels. This disrupts bone growth in children and causes pain and eventual paralysis in the old.

In rich countries, health officials put the "optimum" fluoride dose in water supplies at about 1 part per million. In India, that is regarded as the maximum safe level. But in many Indian villages, it can also be a dangerous level. In one Indian village studied in detail, water with between 0.7

and 1.6 parts per million of fluoride was enough to leave almost a fifth of the population suffering from bent bones and skeletal fluorosis.

■   From Hirapur, I went to nearby Tilaipani, a tiny cattle-rearing hamlet half a mile from the nearest road. A few years ago, cattle drinking from new boreholes sunk by the government started to go lame. Then humans began to suffer, too. It was here in 1995 that Tapas Chakma, a young researcher at the Regional Medical Research Centre in nearby Jabalpur, first uncovered the hidden epidemic of fluorosis across this part of Madhya Pradesh. He suggested that a local girl's strange bone deformities might be caused by fluorosis. Initially, he was rebuffed by officials. "I asked the Pollution Control Board about the water here, and they assured me it was safe," Chakma recalled. "I didn't accept that and sent a water sample to Delhi, which revealed the truth."

Chakma's subsequent studies found cases of severe knock-knees in half of all the children in the village. In many cases, their upper arms and their legs below the knee were splayed outward. The highest rate of deformity, 70 percent, was among 6- to 10-year-olds, who were toddlers when the pumps first replaced surface wells in the village. In the worst cases, Chakma told me, their spines became entirely rigid and their legs so bowed inward that they are permanently crossed.

After his discoveries in Tilaipani, Chakma began to hear about similar problems in other villages across the district of Mandla, which has a population of around a million. He publicly called for a districtwide screening of water pumps so that contaminated wells could be shut down. Since then, engineers have dismantled more than 500 pumps in more than 300 villages in the district to prevent people from drinking the poisoned water.

Since 1996, all the hand pumps in Tilaipani have been shut. Women have resumed their age-old trek to fill buckets from a distant water hole.

As the engineers have shut wells, doctors have revealed that they have been seeing cases of fluoride poisoning among their patients since the late 1980s. But, as with the symptoms of arsenic poisoning in Bangladesh, they did not know what they were seeing. In this remote corner of central India, the doctors say they hadn't heard of fluorosis. When children came to them with limb deformities, they were diagnosed instead with arthritis, polio, rickets, genetic faults, or simply a "mystery disease." The link with water and fluoride was never made until Chakma stumbled on the truth.

When I visited the area, Mandla was still the only district in Madhya Pradesh to have systematically tested its water for fluoride. But since then, its neighbors across the state have started to do tests, with disturbing results. The more the scientists look, the more they find. Dozens of pumps have now been shut in the district of Dindori, for instance. The local press reported panic as engineers took away pump handles without offering an explanation to villagers. In one village in the district, Bichia, water had been found with almost thirteen times the safe limit. The one certainty seems to be that many more such villages will be uncovered in the coming years.

India's fluoride tragedy is a tiny part of a landscape of ignorance, confusion, and indifference that is crippling millions. "Engineers just presume that underground water is clean so they don't test it. Doctors are not taught about fluorosis in our medical schools, so they don't diagnose it," says Andezhath Susheela of the Fluorosis Research and Rural Development Foundation in Delhi. She has been unraveling the national scandal of fluoride in drinking water for a decade, during which time her estimate of the number of people leading "a painful and crippled life" from fluorosis has risen from 1 million, first to 25 million, and now to 60 million. Six million of them are children. "The fluoride problem in India is enormous, unbelievable. In some villages, three-quarters of the population are seriously affected," she says.

Fluoride seems simply to have been forgotten about for many years by those in India responsible for overseeing the country's rural water supplies. Neither doctors nor water engineers can claim there were no clues as to what was happening. The first instances of fluorosis in areas where underground water contained high fluoride levels were recorded in India 60 years ago. As early as 1962, the government's health ministry published a list of hot spots in several states where villagers suffered fluorosis from water. In Madhya Pradesh, government scientists named twelve districts as being at risk in the 1980s. A national task force to educate doctors and engineers was formed in 1986. Gourisankar Ghosh, as head of India's National Drinking Water Mission, personally warned about the problem in the late 1980s, but to little avail. He says today: "There should have been far greater vigilance. We were sinking 60,000 boreholes a year and analyzing water from at most a tenth of them."

The process by which fluoride gets into well water is rather different from how arsenic gets there. Arsenic is brought to Bangladesh and northern India in river water and accumulates in soft river sediments near the surface. Deep wells are usually safe. But fluoride is dissolved directly from the bedrock. In places like Madhya Pradesh, it is the deep wells near this bedrock that run the greatest risk of containing fluoride. In recent years, geologists have established that fluoride gets into water wherever there is granite bedrock. As the bedrock is slowly eroded by natural processes, rich seams of fluoride are often exposed and then dissolved by underground water. The risks are especially high where underground water is low in calcium, which increases the rate at which the fluoride is dissolved, and where the water sits in pores in the bedrock for long periods. All these risk factors apply in Mandla, where the fluoride-bearing water is mostly pumped up from below 180 feet, close to the fluoride-containing bedrock.

The problem seems bound to get worse. India's escalating water crisis is forcing people to search for water deeper and deeper underground. When you pump deeper water, you are tapping older water, water that has been in contact with the bedrock for longer. So it is more contaminated. As the water tables continue to fall, fluoride levels in thousands of wells, many of them still untested, will continue to rise.

According to Ravi Shankar Tiwary, Chakma's boss at the Jabalpur Regional Medical Research Centre, there is an extra tragedy in Mandla. The water tables are usually at around 100 feet. That is well above the fluoride-bearing layers. There was rarely any need to sink the boreholes into the poisoned zones. But private contractors sank boreholes deeper as part of a scam to increased the value of the contracts. The deeper they drilled, the more they were paid. At the same time, Tiwary alleges, Mandla health officials falsely claimed to have tested the water for fluoride. "They said at first that they had tested the water. But they didn't. I know, because they didn't have the right equipment." Officials at the Mandla Department of Public Health Engineering still brush off inquiries. They even rebuff UNICEF, which has sought to repair some of the damage by offering to install some trial defluoridation equipment. "In Mandla, the administration is so terrified they won't let us go near," the agency's water project officer in Delhi told me.

Fluoride, like arsenic, is a worldwide menace. Excessive natural fluoride is present in underground water supplies in at least 20 other countries, according to Gourisankar Ghosh, who now runs UNICEF's worldwide water operations from its New York headquarters. The poison gushes to the surface from Chile to China, where there are an estimated 1.6 million victims, and from Ethiopia to Uzbekistan.

Hand pumps installed during the UN International Water Decade of the 1980s gave villagers control over their own water supply and freed them from reliance on either polluted surface waters or expensive networks of pipes bringing water from distant sources. But the water decade became a race to sink as many wells as possible as quickly as possible. India set its own target of providing at least one source of water for every 250 people. And it declared that no source should be more than a mile from the community it served. Susheela says there was "an obsession with meeting targets." Engineers arrived, sank their wells, and then departed, testing little and leaving no one to oversee the quality of water emerging from the wells. Public health officials were rarely consulted, often didn't even know where the new wells were installed, had little geological knowledge to guide them in seeking out potential problems, and in any case subscribed to the general view that underground water was safe because it was safe from sewage bacteria.

In India, UNICEF sank relatively few wells itself. But it claims to have "set the agenda" for the switch to underground water over the past two decades by formulating plans, promoting pump designs, and encouraging the Indian government to speed up the program and reduce costs by employing private drilling contractors to sink the wells. But it is reluctant to take responsibility for what happened in villages like Hirapur. You have to scan the fine print of the agency's glossy brochures before finding any references to the fluoride problems. In a recent fifty-page booklet on UNICEF's water work in India, fluoride merited just two paragraphs.

However, officials on the ground do now privately admit their errors. "Yes, it became a numbers game," says Rupert Talbot, head of water policy for UNICEF in Delhi until mid-2003. "When you are driven by demand, quality is inclined to slip. Contractors got away with murder." This blind pursuit of development targets lost sight of the welfare of the people that the development was designed to help. Hydrological goals had replaced human goals. It was, Talbot says, never possible for government officials to check whether boreholes were sunk to the right depth, were protected from pollution, or had their water tested on completion. He estimates that at least one hand pump in every ten in India today is contaminated with unsafe levels of natural chemicals, mostly fluoride and arsenic.

Many water specialists now argue that surface water sources should not have been so wantonly abandoned. Rather, they should have been renovated and made safe. Even UNICEF is now having a change of heart. Talbot says: "I think there is a lot to be said for sticking with the old water sources, such as shallow wells and rainwater harvesting, provided they can be made safer, for instance by keeping animals away." What an admission.

Clearly, in India and elsewhere, the hand pumps of the International Water Decade brought real benefits to millions of people. They can take a large share of the credit for a dramatic reduction in cases of dysentery and of parasites such as guinea worm, which once infested many open wells but is now virtually eradicated from the country. But the wholesale promotion of hand pumps as a cheap panacea to meet ambitious international targets has in many places proved disastrous. As Vishwas Joshi, UNICEF's water project officer in Delhi, puts it: "More enthusiasm for water quality and less for a pursuit of quantity at all costs would have left many more people with safe drinking water today." Thousands of children limping around their villages would agree.

CHAPTER NINE

A Salty Hell

Hollow-cheeked and emaciated, her head wrapped in a scarf, the woman shuffled along the grubby corridor of the Muynak fish cannery. In the 1960s, this place was the showpiece of a large Soviet fishing industry on the Aral Sea in Central Asia. The sea was so rich that the sailors on the trawlers, which brought ashore 50,000 tons of fish a year, were regularly featured on Soviet propaganda films. But we were now in the late 1990s. The woman edged past large paintings from the glory days. They showed more heroic workers turning those fish into canned protein for distribution across the Soviet empire. She grasped a handrail hard as she inched her way into a cavernous canning room, a pitiful reminder of busier days.

She seemed oblivious of the foreign visitors, me among them, standing on the stairs. We had stayed on after attending an international conference being held in Karakalpakstan, a semi-independent republic of the Central Asian state of Uzbekistan, where women without the strength to lift their feet are a common sight. It is a poisoned land—a place and people devastated more by large dams and insane water management policies than probably anywhere else on Earth.

Karakalpakstan was from the first a spooky place. Virtually the entire population of Nukus, the capital, lined the streets as we drove in from the airport to the conference. Foreigners rarely come here. Now that they had, the main hotel had been spruced up, and the streets were washed from large water trucks at dawn to keep the dust down. It was only in the days after the conference was over, when the handful of remaining delegates were free to move around and the authorities seemed to think we had disappeared altogether, that some truths began to emerge. The beer ran out. So, more alarmingly, did the water in the hotel taps. Water that a day before had seemed so plentiful that they could wash the streets with it was now so scarce that even the top hotel couldn't get any.

The conference had been held to discuss the disappearance of the Aral Sea. Notoriously, the sea has gone because Soviet engineers a generation ago decided to capture the waters of the two giant rivers that fed it—the Syr Darya and the Amu Darya, which has been known for most of recorded history as the Oxus. For several decades, the water irrigated the fields that grew the cotton that clothed the Soviet Union.

You don't have to go to Karakalpakstan to see the breathtaking consequences of this massive exercise in geoengineering. Anyone taking a flight from Europe to Southeast Asia, as I have, and using one of those maps at the back of the airline magazines to follow the route, can get an inkling of the scale of what has been done. There are few landmarks in Central Asia, but on a bright and clear moonlit night, I spotted the railway line from Moscow to Tashkent, the capital of Uzbekistan. Looking for a town, I finally picked out the lights of Aralsk, a port that sat, the airline map assured me, on the northern shore of the Aral Sea. Except that it wasn't on any shore. Instead of waves washing up to the town's harbor and promenade, I saw a vast expanse of barren desert, glinting white in the moonlight. The shoreline itself was more than 40 miles to the south, and the white expanse that filled the gap was salt: crystals of calcium carbonate, sodium chloride, sodium sulphate, and magnesium chloride left behind as the sea had dried up.

The Aral Sea drains an area of around 250,000 square miles. Its basin consists of mountains, harsh deserts, and dry steppe from the Hindu Kush in Afghanistan to the borders of Russia. Until half a century ago, the Amu Darya and Syr Darya between them carried around 100 million acre-feet of water a year out of the mountains—more than flows down the Nile in Africa. In the desert heat, half of this water evaporated; but the remainder made it to the Aral Sea, maintaining it as the world's fourth-largest inland sea. However, from around 1957, as Soviet planners began creating their cotton empire in what was then called Soviet Central Asia, they began to remove so much water from the rivers that the Aral Sea began to dry up. The last trawler was left to rot on the disappearing shore in 1984. Delta regions at the mouths of the great rivers that had once run with wild boar, deer, enough muskrats to allow a harvest of 650,000 pelts in 1960, and even the occasional tiger were reduced to arid scrub.

The area of irrigated lands in Central Asia doubled between 1950 and 1988 to some 19 million acres. Down here, they called the Russian technocrats "Commissar Cotton" for their single-minded devotion to turning these arid lands into cotton fields. "Commissar Cotton" turned nations of cowboys into cotton pickers.

■ Cotton is a very thirsty crop. Typically, Soviet planners poured 5 feet of water a year onto their cotton fields. It was the equivalent of filling a chest-high lake across an area the size of Scotland. There was little left for the Aral Sea, which though an inland sea without any outlets was by now losing far more water to evaporation than it gained each year from the paltry flows that made it down the rivers. By the late 1980s, it was receiving just 4 million acre-feet a year, a tenth of the natural flow. The sea's surface area halved to less than 13,000 square miles; its volume shrank by more than two-thirds; and its salinity tripled. Even since the collapse of the Soviet Union, after which the nations of the basin publicly dedicated themselves to replenishing the sea, it has continued to shrink. By 2003, it was reduced to two small seas with a combined surface area only a quarter of the old sea's.

The key to the collapse of the sea was probably the construction of the Karakum Canal, which for the first time took water entirely outside the Aral Sea basin and into the catchment of the Caspian Sea to the west. At 800 miles, the Karakum Canal is the longest irrigation canal in the world. It is also one of the largest in capacity. It alone took 13 million acre-feet of water a year from the Amu Darya, making it almost as large a waterway as the Colorado River. In 30 years, the Karakum Canal has abstracted 180 million acre-feet of water, roughly the same as the entire volume of the Aral Sea today. Most of the water has been used by the now-independent Republic of Turkmenistan, which has the dubious claim of using more water per citizen than any other nation on Earth. Cotton remains its main crop.

While cotton is thirsty, however, it is not that thirsty. The hydrological inefficiency of irrigation in Central Asia is staggering. Irrigation engineers have simply wasted huge amounts of the region's precious water. In places, at least half the water in irrigation canals seeps into the sand. And half of what is left is poured onto already waterlogged fields. Most of this surplus eventually evaporates in the sun, leaving its salt behind as a white sprinkling, disconcertingly like snow. But a flight from Uzbekistan's capital, Tashkent, west toward the Aral Sea reveals where the rest ends up. Not far west of Tashkent, on the edge of a large irrigated area, is a huge lake some

100 miles long and 7 miles wide. It's not on any map, though it does have
a name. Lake Aydarkul is composed entirely of surplus water overflowing
from decrepit irrigation works and waterlogged fields. Farther west, on the
border between Turkmenistan and Karakalpakstan, is another even larger
overflow lake. Sarykamysh in some years receives more water than the
Aral Sea itself. And everywhere near the irrigated fields there are other,
smaller lakes. Many are sufficiently permanent to have local names.

The situation is even more bizarre in Turkmenistan, destination for the
flows of the Karakum Canal. Here, much of the water stolen from the Aral
Sea basin sits today in a saline lake covering more than 300 square miles.
The desert capital of Ashkhabad is surrounded by swamps made largely of
the canal's water. Turkmenistan has so much water flowing off its fields that
the megalomaniac president Saparmurat Niyazov wants to create a brand
new permanent lake in the Karakum Desert to commemorate his rule. It
will be called the Golden Century Lake—a fitting testimony indeed.

Most irrigation systems around the world have complex networks of
drains to remove some of the unwanted water and chemicals from the
fields and channel it back into rivers or take it direct to the sea. But the
Russians never got around to digging drains here. So the basin is now pep-
pered with impromptu sumps in natural depressions. "I don't think that
the total area of surface water in the Aral Basin is any less than in the
1950s," said Jan Post of the World Bank during the conference. "It is just
that most of it is no longer in the Aral Sea." The irony is harsh. While the
region has a desperate shortage of water, fields and desert hollows are
choked with the stuff, in the form of useless toxic brine.

At one stage in this sorry saga, Soviet planners seem to have decided to
make a virtue out of what they saw as necessity. They decided that emptying the Aral Sea was no bad thing. In the 1960s, one former president of

the Academy of Sciences in Turkmenistan declared: "I belong to those scientists who consider that drying up the Aral Sea is far more advantageous
than preserving it. Good fertile land will be obtained. Cultivation of cotton alone [on the seabed] will pay for the existing Aral Sea with its fisheries, shipping, and other industries." A science commission set up in 1975
concluded without demur that "current practice . . . foreordains the reduction of the Aral Sea to a small, saturated salt solution."

But not everyone agreed. In the 1980s, a head of steam developed
behind the idea of diverting north-flowing Siberian rivers across the
steppe to relieve the beleaguered sea and provide yet more water for irrigation. The Ob and the Irtysh between them have flows of 350 million
acre-feet a year, so even allowing for big losses to evaporation and seepage
along the proposed 1,500-mile canal, a small proportion would have been
enough. The plan attracted international opprobrium, however. Some scientists warned that it could cause global climate change. And Russian
nationalists also opposed annexing "their" rivers. The scheme was finally
scuppered by Mikhail Gorbachev months before the collapse of the Soviet
Union put to flight all thought of such fraternal endeavor to relieve the
plight of Russia's neighbors.

■ Irrigation has transformed the geochemistry as well as the hydrology
of the Aral Basin. The mismanagement of water is in considerable part
responsible for the excessive salt content of drinking water in the Aral
Basin. All rivers carry salt, dissolved from rocks in the headwaters and
from salty deposits downstream. Most of this water is normally discharged into the sea. But in the Aral Basin, most is diverted with the irrigation water onto fields, where it accumulates.

And now a vicious cycle kicks in. To prevent the salt from poisoning crops, farmers pour on more water to wash the salt away from the root zone. This works for a few crucial weeks to allow a new crop to grow. But as the new water evaporates, it leaves the soil more salty and waterlogged than ever. So each year, more water is added than the year before—and more salt is left behind. But eventually even the flushing fails. Around 3 million acres of cotton fields in Uzbekistan have already been abandoned to salt and waterlogging. In Karakalpakstan, one in five fields has been abandoned, and the productivity of those that are left has halved since the 1970s. Soviet planners inadvertently stumbled on a foolproof system for creating deserts, and though the planners are long gone, the processes of desertification continue.

The fields are filled with salt from another source, too—the 14,000 square miles of exposed seabed, where the salt of an entire sea has ended up in saline dust. Amid the rough scrub and sand dunes of perhaps the largest dust bowl in the whole of Asia, there are extensive salt pans, which are visible from the air as blinding white patches. And across this salty wasteland, stiff winds blow each winter. The United Nations estimates that 75 million tons of salt enter the atmosphere annually from the Aral Sea bed during these dust storms. And the fallout on former coastal towns like Muynak is put at a quarter-ton per acre per year.

Winds that once brought moisture from the sea now bring only lethal dust that destroys soils, blankets vegetation, and gets into food and water supplies. Cosmonauts taking off from the nearby Baikonur launchpad can watch the dust storms from orbit. The aberrant chemistry of the dusty fallout can be measured as far away as the Arctic Circle and the River Ganges in India. It spreads as perniciously as the radioactivity from the nuclear testing ground at Semipalatinsk, another local enterprise. And with the salts comes pesticides—the residues of some of the most intense applications of farm chemicals attempted anywhere in the world. At the peak of chemical applications, in the late 1980s, before cash shortages imposed their own restrictions, a typical acre of cotton fields in Central Asia received more than 300 pounds of fertilizer annually and 120 pounds of pesticides. Many of the formulations, like the lethal butifos, a defoliant, have since been banned. But that is of no consolation to the people of Karakalpakstan, who still breathe in the deadly dust whenever the wind crosses the steppe from the seabed.

Every aspect of the environment in Karakalpakstan and beyond is suffused with salt. While most people have heard about the ecological havoc from the draining of the Aral Sea, many fewer have heard of the pandemics caused among the human population by this mass poisoning with salt. The woman shuffling white-knuckled up the stairs of the canning factory, a mockery of the heroic pictures on the walls, was one out of a nation of anemics.

Of the 700,000 women who live in the tiny republic, 97 percent are clinically anemic, says Oral Ataniyazova, a local doctor who has campaigned for more attention to be given to their plight. This is almost certainly the highest rate of anemia anywhere in the world. The women also suffer from rising rates of kidney and thyroid disease, and from throat, stomach, and liver cancers. Karakalpakstan has the highest rate of cancer of the esophagus in the world. Over the past 15 years, there has been an increase in the rates of allergies, tuberculosis, and birth defects. Pregnant women attending the maternity hospital are routinely given iron supplements to combat the anemia. But it barely helps. "Their bodies simply cannot absorb the iron," says Ataniyazova, who has treated mothers and their children here for almost two decades. "All of our women are sick."

Four out of five children are born anemic. One in twenty has a congenital disorder. Infant mortality exceeds 80 per thousand live births in places, three times the average for Uzbekistan, and easily the highest rate in the former Soviet Union. "Increasing numbers of children have damaged immune systems," said the director of the overflowing children's hospital in Nukus. "The sick children are almost all born to sick mothers." Nor are the men spared: one in five is rejected as unfit for Uzbeki national service. In parts of Karakalpakstan, life expectancy is 20 years less than the average for the former Soviet Union. Everybody who can get out is fleeing this health crisis. The population of the old fishing port and canning town of Muynak today is 27,000, half what it was in 1960.

"It's the water that makes them sick," say the doctors with resignation. The only drinking water available for most people is polluted drainage water from fields upstream, full of salt and farm chemicals from irrigated fields. The underground water ultimately comes from the same place and is no better than the surface water. That is all anyone has to drink. In Muynak, the water coming out of the municipal pipes contains sixteen times more salt than the limit set by the World Health Organization. "The salt content is so high that milk curdles in your tea," says Ataniyazova. "We have searched the scientific literature but can find no research into a health situation like this anywhere else in the world."

In the desert around the Aral Sea, all life depends on drainage water. People drink it. Their grapes, melons, and vegetables soak it up. So do their cattle and sheep, and the few remaining diseased fish farmed in polluted lagoons of the Amu Darya Delta and sent to the canning factory. I asked fishermen at Ushay, a tiny, desolate fishing village of timber and mud shacks in the midst of the desiccated delta, why they still caught such obviously poisoned catches. One shrugged: "What should we do? It's not just the fish. We are all polluted."

■   The emptying of the Aral Sea and the disaster around it are an environmental holocaust. One of the word's great inland seas has been reduced to a drainage sump in the vast hot desert wilderness of Central Asia. But while the world has become familiar with pictures of the departed Aral Sea and the wrecks of fishing vessels amid sand dunes, this is in truth yesterday's crisis. Few people in Karakalpakstan, or in the Kyzl Orda region on the sea's northern shores in Kazakhstan, have seen the Aral Sea since it slipped over the horizon some 30 years ago. When locals joined foreign journalists on a plane ride from the tiny airport in Nukus to find the sea, they were themselves aghast at the sheer scale of what has happened here. But it is the salinization of Central Asia resulting from the misuse of the region's water and the loss of its sea that is the greater threat to the inhabitants. It is salt that is destroying the region's economy, ecology, and health.

Will the region and its sea ever recover? Kazakhstan is making efforts to save some part of what is now called the North Aral Sea by reducing its surface area still further to reduce evaporation. But the South Aral Sea in Uzbekistan, which is about to divide into two pools, has to all intents and purposes been abandoned to its fate. In 2002, government scientists in Uzbekistan briefly resurrected the idea of diverting north-flowing Siberian rivers across the Russian steppes to refill their sea. "There is no other way to address this problem but to source water outside this region," Ismail Jurabekov, an aide to the long-standing Uzbek president Islam Karimov told an international conference. Russia wants nothing to do with the idea. So what else?

There are two basic reasons why the Aral Sea is empty: the region's addiction to the cotton economy and its inefficient use of water. Neither shows any sign of being tackled effectively. Inertia and the maintenance of the current poisonous status quo seem to dominate events. And the people of Karakalpakstan, stuck in a small semiautonomous and politically powerless republic within Uzbekistan, have no voice and no influence.

Cotton production transcends all other national goals. In Uzbekistan, the cotton business still amounts to 60 percent of exports and employs 40 percent of the workforce—as well as consuming 90 percent of its water. During the three-month cotton-picking season, schools shut throughout the republic, and work gangs round up young and old for the fields. Entire communities are press-ganged to bring home the crop on the state-run farms, for all the world as if "Commissar Cotton" had never gone home. Even hospitals, according to some Western reports, are ransacked for potential laborers.

The newly independent Central Asian republics talk from time to time about improving the efficiency of irrigation and converting some land to growing grains, which the Soviet system once required them to import. There is an agreed target to cut water use in the Aral Sea basin by a quarter in 20 years, but no concrete plan for carrying this out. Meanwhile, the republics simply maintain the interrepublic agreements on sharing the waters first imposed by Stalin.

Engineers have drawn up plans to drain the fields and desert sumps to refill the sea. This would provide some relief for the Aral Sea in the short term while more gradual reforms to agriculture take place. But the costs would be high. And neither international donors, who have grown weary of corrupt and inefficient government in the region, nor the governments themselves seem keen on the plan. If only by default, they seem to have largely written off the Aral Sea, and perhaps with it the lands and peoples around it. Hydrologists like Peter Zavialov of the Shorshov Institute of Oceanography in Moscow believe the sea will be entirely gone by 2020.

Among the saddest moments during my visit to Nukus were the constant refrains of children asking for a return of their sea. Their classrooms were full of paintings of a sea that most could only imagine from the stories of their parents. One student delegate was allowed to address the conference of government ministers, scientists, UN officials, and World Bank fund-raisers. He had a simple message: "We want to see sea, rather than sand. Every year conferences are held, but we see no actual results." Nobody among the assembled dignitaries was honest enough to tell him the truth. There are no plans to bring back the Aral Sea. There is no scheme to end the bitter harvest of salt in this blighted land.

■ Projects like Commissar Cotton's remaking of Central Asia were Russia's answer to the New Deal in the United States. But if the aims of Roosevelt's United States and Stalin's USSR were similar in terms of their desire to conquer nature, Stalin's methods showed a brutality to the landscape that matched his brutality to his people. Zeev Wolfson, a senior Soviet official who smuggled a manuscript titled "The Destruction of Nature in the Soviet Union" to the West in the 1970s, noted that "the more such projects contradicted the laws of nature, the more highly they were regarded, the more brilliantly the illusion of their success demonstrated the power and wisdom of the new leaders." But seldom has the spirit of the modernist age been so brilliantly and brutally expressed as by a leading Soviet writer in the 1920s, Vladimir Zazubrin, who wrote: "Let the fragile green breast . . . be dressed in the cement armor of cities, armed with the stone muzzles of factory chimneys, and girded with iron belts of railroads. Let the taiga be burned and felled, let the steppes be trampled. Let this be, and so it will be inevitably. Only in cement and iron can the fraternal union of all peoples, the iron brotherhood of all mankind be forged."

In the late 1940s, after victory in the Second World War, Stalin launched his Great Plan for the Transformation of Nature, with plans to build great hydroelectric dams to power industrial development on the Volga and Dnieper Rivers, which flow south through Russia into the Caspian and Black Seas, respectively. The Americans were building most of their dams in gorges, to collect the most water and generate the most power from the least loss of land. But Soviet engineers ignored such natural features. They worried little about drowning wide, fertile valleys with shallow reservoirs. And in all they eventually flooded an area roughly the size of France.

Typical was the Kuibyshev Dam on the Volga, finished in 1953 and declared by Stalin to be Russia's answer to the Grand Coulee Dam. It created Europe's largest man-made lake, a swamp-fringed mass of water more than 300 miles long and up to 25 miles wide. But so poor was its ability to generate electricity that it flooded the equivalent of half a soccer field to produce a single kilowatt of power. Around the same time, the Tsimlyansk Dam was completed on the valley of the River Don. It flooded a thousand square miles of rich farmland, drowning two soccer fields for every kilowatt of energy produced. Wolfson calculated that in many of Stalin's hydroprojects, if the land had been planted with hay rather than flooded, the annual harvest could have been burned to produce more energy than the hydroelectric plant did.

Stalin's Soviet Union perpetrated some of the worst hydrological disasters the world has ever seen. Their descendants will live with the consequences for centuries to come. Perhaps we will never see their like again. But as China and India begin their mega-engineering projects to remake their nations, we cannot be too sure. Certainly the consequences of their failure could be just as horrendous as those today visited on Karakalpakstan.

PART III

The Keepers

CHAPTER TEN

The Last of a Dying Breed?

Yannis Mitsis is an unlikely water diviner. A 65-year-old shoemaker and farmer, he lives in a small village in Cyprus, an arid Mediterranean island where most rivers are dry for six months of the year. But he is reputedly the last man left on the island who knows how to summon water from the depths of the hillside, using nothing more than a pickax, a tripod, and gravity. Squat, gray-haired, and smiling, he hardly seems like a man who in his younger years was a convicted killer, after fighting for what he saw as the Greek cause on this divided island.

I met him one spring day at his modest home among the vegetable gardens and almond groves of the small village of Peristerona—a dozen miles west of the capital city, Nicosia, and only a couple of miles from the border that now divides Greek and Turkish Cyprus. He served coffee, introduced me to his wife, and showed me photographs of his son. Outside, the land was divided between the dry scrub away from the villages and the lush ground close by. It was already baking hot in the coastal resorts of southern Cyprus, but we could see away on the horizon that ice was still melting in the mountains of the island's interior. The rivers were empty, but clearly the meltwater was going somewhere. It was going underground, where Mitsis would catch it.

Mitsis learned from his father the ancient craft of capturing the underground water and taking it to the fields and orchards of his village through systems of tunnels that locals call *laoumia*. These tunnels are in some respects very like the spring-flow tunnels of Israel and Palestine that we discussed in the Introduction, but they are generally longer and are excavated from soft sediments rather than hard rock.

That morning Mitsis described for me how he and his ancestors had made them. The first task, he said, was to dig a "mother well." This was like a conventional well, sunk to the depth of the water table. But instead of allowing farmers to laboriously haul water up from the well, the mother well became the start of a tunnel that followed a slight downhill gradient to take water all the way to the village fields. "From the mother well, we surveyed a tunnel route to the fields where the water would eventually reach the surface," he said. Then they began digging, starting from the exit point and gradually approaching the mother well. Every 30 yards or so, they connected the tunnel to the surface with a further well, to provide ventilation and allow human access, both to remove excavated soil and, later, for maintenance. During construction, and later for repairs, Mitsis would lower himself down the wells and into the tunnels using a pulley system suspended from a wooden tripod erected at the surface. Meanwhile, during excavation, the tunnels were kept straight by lighting candles inside the tunnel and ensuring that they all remained visible during digging.

In the 1940s, when he was 12 years old, Mitsis first began working in the tunnels around his village, carrying earth to the surface. It was hard work. It took five people 15 days to dig a single shaft and 30-yard tunnel section, so one tunnel could take several years to complete. And it was dangerous work. Mitsis's father died when a rope broke while he was repairing a well. But that didn't stop the son from continuing the trade and running his own risks. Mitsis remembers extending a tunnel in the 1940s that passed just a few feet beneath a riverbed, with the ever-present risk of drowning if the tunnel roof broke.

But it was also privileged work, especially for a young boy. There was no higher calling in the village, he remembers. "Water is power here, as important as land. Land without water is next to useless, and for centuries the tunnels have been the source of the water. The Turkish landholders would get together to build, employing masters like my father and workers like me. They had a constant program of digging new tunnels." One, coming in from the east and built about 90 years ago, was known as the "40 tunnel" because it had 40 owners, each entitled to its water for 6 hours every 10 days.

The village's five laoumia supplied all the farms, and others passed beneath the village en route to the neighboring village of Zozia. The longest tunnel extended more than 3 miles and took 7 years to dig. "This was a village of milk and honey. Thanks to the tunnels we never suffered from drought here," said Mitsis.

Mitsis has worked all over Cyprus digging and repairing tunnels, from the western tip, through Nicosia, which until recently was largely supplied with water from two large tunnels, to the far eastern "panhandle." He remembers that in his youth, there used to be three master tunnel builders in his area, including his father. But all are now dead. His family worked as a team. "In times of drought, it was the only work going," he remembers. "That's when everyone would remember the tunnels and commission repairs and new digging. We would work in family teams of five, with two young people carrying earth in the tunnel, one adult digger, and two more people pulling earth up from the wells."

Mitsis dug his last new laoumia in 1954, but he has repaired the existing tunnels ever since. As recently as the early 1990s, he renovated an entire section beneath a field of cactuses and fig trees after a tunnel collapse. He worked alone, lowering himself as much as 200 feet down access wells into the tunnels.

Many of the tunnels are failing now because boreholes sunk by farmers have lowered the water table so much that the mother wells have run dry. In essence, individuals with the most money to sink the deepest wells can now rob the rest of the community of their water. Villagers say the old sense of a community working together to make best use of the local resources, such as water, is disappearing with the laoumia. Yes, of course, the old landlords used to have first right to the water from the tunnels that they had paid to be dug. But in those days, a committee of local farmers distributed the rights to the water and everyone got a share. Now, whenever a tunnel's flow fails, its shafts are capped in concrete, and it is abandoned.

When I met Mitsis in the late 1990s, the committee of village farmers still sent him underground each year to make running repairs to the one tunnel that still watered village orchards. He took me on a tour of his domain, through a landscape of cactuses, dry stone walls, and almond trees. Down the road outside Orounda, there are several more tunnels. One, locally called Maouchos, has beautiful stonework surrounding the mother well—its makers were artists as well as craftsmen. And, just below the mother well, the tunnel divided in two, one arm going on underground to the village while another came to the surface to irrigate fields in a small valley. Mitsis remembered repairing the tunnel here years ago after a collapse in a fava bean field. The tunnels still provide water for most of the year. The village committee charges the local farmers $4,000 a year to pay for repairs.

At the nearby village of Ergates, which has six functioning laoumia, I was directed to a tunnel a mile long that still yields around 250 gallons of water a minute to irrigate fields. An old villager there remembered, "The laoumia was last extended in 1920, and 85 people worked on it." Across the border, in Turkish Cyprus, there are many more tunnels, especially in the area around the town of Morphou. Some were worked on by Mitsis. But he won't talk about them, and he certainly has no prospect of crossing the fortified border to see them.

Cyprus is populated by ethnic Greeks and Turks. Back in the 1940s, when Mitsis began his career, his village in central Cyprus was Turkish owned. But there followed conflicts between the Greeks, the Turks, and the British colonial authorities on the island that led eventually to its division into Greek and Turkish enclaves. The Turkish landowners left the village, and the Greek villagers took over both the tunnels and the land. During this time, Mitsis was one of a band of right-wing Greek nationalists who opposed the plan by then-president Archbishop Makarios to create an independent Cyprus when the British occupiers left. Mitsis was imprisoned by the British during the late 1960s for his murderous exploits. In these villages, the conflict was as much about water as anything. The arid land hereabouts was virtually worthless without water from the laoumia, and where Mitsis lived, it was the Turks who had ultimate control of the water. After the country was divided in the late 1970s, many villages were abandoned, and the tunnels with them.

Because the construction of laoumia has usually been in the hands of peasant farmers, there are few written records of the work. There seem to be no descriptions in English of the laoumia of Cyprus—even though the country was for many decades run by the British at a time when many farmers relied on them for irrigation. And there are only brief notes, in Greek, in government archives in Nicosia. Mitsis, as well as being the last practitioner of this ancient craft on the island, is also its last technical expert—the last man, indeed, to know where many of the tunnels run. After showing off his tunneling equipment for me, he emerged from one last tunnel, folded up his tripod, and went back to his shoemaking. "There is nobody to take my place when I finish," he said. "My son is a criminal lawyer in London. When I stop work, there will be nobody left to repair the tunnels."

CHAPTER ELEVEN

Hidden Wonders
of the Ancient World

Yannis Mitsis is one of a decreasing band of people worldwide who are skilled in a secret art that few modern water engineers would know how to attempt—digging gently sloping tunnels for sometimes tens of miles to bring hidden water to fields and orchards at the surface. They are, in effect, creating underground rivers. These rivers go by many different names. They are called *laoumia* in Cyprus, *foggara* in North Africa, *karez* in Afghanistan, *aflaj* in the Arabian Peninsula, *surangam* in parts of India; and in Iran, where they originated and where they are found in greatest numbers, the Persian word is *qanat*. In some respects, they resemble the spring tunnels of Palestine. But spring tunnels are dug in hard rock and are, by comparison, quite short. Qanats are generally much longer and are dug in loose sediments and broken rock.

Underground water is the largest reservoir of unfrozen freshwater on the planet's surface. Some has been there for millennia; some is just passing through on the way to rivers and the ocean. But all can be tapped, most usefully from aquifers, areas of rock saturated by underground water. Aquifers get their water from the surface, as water percolates down from soils, lakes, or rivers. They release water back to the surface through springs.

Humans have always tapped rivers and springs, of course. But in many parts of the world, there are few of these that discharge water all year round. And in such places, we have gone excavating for water.

Westerners are familiar with wells and with their mechanized equivalent, the borehole. Wells and boreholes, however, require power—whether human, animal, or mechanical—to bring water to the surface. That is fine for drinking water, but expensive for providing water to irrigate crops except where, as we saw in India, the electricity for pumping is heavily subsidized. So in many parts of the arid and mountainous world, communities have come up with novel systems of tunnels that penetrate into hillsides to tap underground water and bring it to the surface while maintaining a shallow gradient. Gravity does the hard work.

Qanats were first dug about 3,000 years ago in ancient Persia, modern-day Iran. Most rain falls high in the mountains here, but there are few rivers rushing out of the mountains. Most of the rain and melting winter snow percolates from the high rockfaces into the huge accumulations of broken rock and sediment that shroud the lower slopes of the mountains. If the water emerges at all, it is in small springs on the valley floors far below. But the Persians learned to maximize the meager flows from these springs by digging horizontal tunnels into the hillsides where the springs emerged. They found that the farther back they dug, the more water the springs delivered, and the greater its reliability.

What probably began as a smart idea to help peasants get through a dry spell turned into the wellspring for farming societies across Persia. At one time, qanat digging in Persia must have been one of the biggest civil engineering enterprises on the planet, easily on a par with the construction of the Egyptian pyramids. The engineering statistics are truly extraordinary. There are an estimated 40,000 qanats in modern Iran alone. End to end, they would reach two-thirds of the way to the moon, and their total discharge as recently as the 1960s was put at more than 5 million gallons of water a second, equivalent to the flow of eight River Niles.

One giant tunnel near Gonabad in eastern Iran is wide enough for a horse to gallop through and has a mother well at its head that is more than a thousand feet deep. If these structures were above ground, they would be among the great wonders of the world and visited by millions. As it is, they are barely known about, even in Iran. There are no World Heritage Site listings, no international appeals for repairs or conservation, and few efforts to keep up the craft skills that could maintain the tunnels.

Qanats have maintained Persia for many centuries. When the Mongol hordes invaded Persia some 800 years ago and destroyed many qanats, the resulting loss of water caused widespread famine and, historians have argued, a long-term drop in the Persian population. Recovery came only when new tunnels were dug. Even today, according to one of the modern qanat historians, Paul Ward English of the University of Texas at Austin, more than 5 million acres of fields and orchards are still irrigated from qanats. Qanats power many village water mills and provide water for sacred pools inside mosques. But in rural areas, the main function of qanats is to irrigate fields and orchards.

Typically, qanats have hundreds of owners, and the water may be divided into thousands of time-shares. Many of the participants get their water rights in return for carrying out repairs to the structures. Often there are ancient and detailed rules about who gets what water when, with equally ancient offices of water bailiffs to oversee the sharing out. In Ardistan in central Iran, the division of waters goes back to the 1200s, when Hulagu Khan, the grandson of Genghis Khan, ordered that the water be divided into twenty-one shares, each allotted to a specific quarter.

In ancient Persia, qanats always watered cities as well as farms. They filled the fountains of the palace cities of Persepolis and Palmyra in 500 BC. Until the 1930s, three dozen large tunnels and more than a hundred small tunnels supplied Tehran with most of its water from the nearby Ulburz Mountains. One even gushed its water into the grounds of the British Embassy. As late as the 1970s, qanats were the main water supply for Isfahan, a city of more than a million people. One ancient tunnel supplying the city was more than 50 miles long. The city of Irbil still uses qanats built by King Sennacherib 2,700 years ago. Nineveh in modern Mosul, northern Iraq, was watered with qanats after the Assyrian king Sargon II discovered the technology in Iran.

The modern-day Iranian capital of qanats is the ancient city of Yazd, where qanats even have a museum devoted to them. The city is an architectural marvel above ground. It is a major center for the Persian wind towers that provide ventilation for houses through turrets oriented toward the prevailing valley winds, for instance. But below ground there is more. Yazd's qanats bring water into the desert city from the surrounding mountains, such as the 13,000-foot-high Mount Sir. In all, the valley boasts around 2,500 qanats. From the air, their routes can be seen clearly on the desert floor, marked by the pockmarks of the heads of the regularly spaced access wells. The longest, the Dowlat Abad qanat, is more than 40 miles long. Some mother wells here are a thousand feet deep. Within the city itself, the qanats follow the street patterns and supply public cisterns at intersections, so that spare water never goes to waste.

■ Qanat technology spread with the Persians as they conquered their neighbors. Between 500 BC and AD 600 this technology spread west through the Middle East, along the African shores of the Mediterranean,

Discoverer of the spring tunnels: Israeli geographer Zvi Ron.

Palestinian Ahmad Qot takes water from an ancient spring tunnel at Madamaon in the West Bank.

Winners and losers: water gushes into the Kano Irrigation Project in
northern Nigeria, but downstream wetlands dry up as a result.

Gadaffi's pipes irrigate Libya's fields with ancient water from beneath the
Sahara. (© Galen R. Frysinger.)

Elaborate dug wells like this one in Tamil Nadu, India,
have been emptied by plunging water tables.

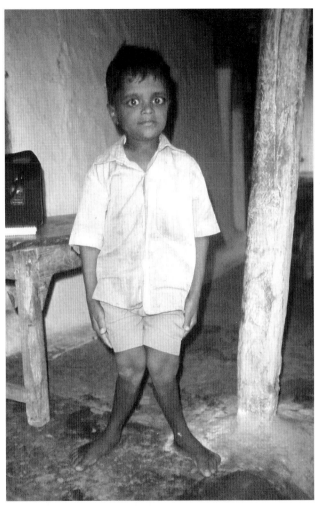

Shatap's deformed legs are caused by drinking well water
contaminated with fluoride.

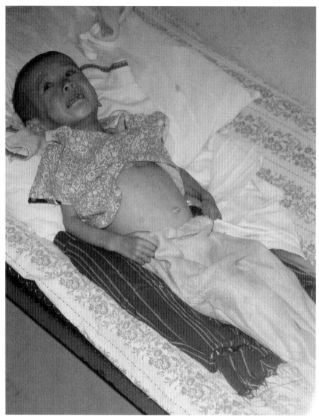

Close to death in the children's hospital of the salt-poisoned
town of Nukus near the shrivelled Aral Sea.

Yannis Mitsis, the last qanat digger in Cyprus, displays his equipment.

A sluice gate regulates underground water delivered to
a Cypriot village from an ancient tunnel.

Like a Persian qanat, a karez delivers these waters to an Afghan field.

Time-honored tradition: irrigation of rice paddies on ancient hill terraces in southeast Asia. (© UNESCO/D. Roger.)

Hadeja's miracle: water flows throughout the dry season
in Rajasamadhiya, thanks to harvesting the rain.

Water harvesting: goats and people share this
precious pond in India's Thar desert.

Traditional water storage in the Indian desert city of Jodhpur.

Turning the tide of history: Jane Ngei's bucket and hose irrigation
in Machakos, Kenya.

An array of fog catchers on a hillside in Chile's Atacama desert.
(© Bob Schemenauer, FogQuest.)

and east along the old Silk Road to China. It traveled with Persian invaders but usually long outlasted them. There are qanats still in use in southern Afghanistan, Pakistan, western China, Cyprus, Egypt, Yemen, Oman, and the Kurdish lands of Iraq. Recent excavations have found hundreds of tunnels stretching for thousands of miles beneath the Libyan Desert, relics of the lost civilization of Garamantes, a tribe of oasis dwellers who lived in northern Libya during Roman times. And Arabs, having adopted the technology themselves, took qanat digging on into Morocco, Algeria, and Spain, where qanats watered Moorish Madrid, and even to the Canary Islands, far out in the Atlantic Ocean. Today, qanats remain the mainstay of peasant agriculture in the Algerian Sahara. They are the major source of irrigation water for the fields and towering hillside terraces that occupy the mountains of the Arabian Peninsula, where they have for some 2,000 years allowed villagers to grow wheat and alfalfa for their cattle. Oman has 11,000 tunnels, almost half of which still have permanent flows of water running from their mouths. Here, as in most areas where qanats are still in use, the complex social organization of many villages is built around the cooperative use and maintenance of the aflaj and their water.

In the Turfan Valley in the vast, arid region of northwest China, a total of 3,000 miles of karez, built during the Han and Qing dynasties, still tap water from the Bogdashan Mountains and sustain vineyards in desert oases. The longest tunnels extend more than 7 miles. In Turfan, they speak of China's three great engineering marvels: the Great Wall, the imperial Grand Canal—and the karez. Despite the spread of modern pumps, karez still provide a third of all the water used in the region.

Few descriptions of this huge water supply infrastructure ever reach the textbooks of Western water engineers. So when American engineers went to Afghanistan after the 2001 war, they were amazed to discover that karez were indispensable to irrigation in many areas distant from rivers in the south of the country. After the 2003 invasion of Iraq, American engineers found a similar story in the Kurdish territories of the north, where the town of Sulaimaniya still makes heavy use of its qanats.

Throughout central Asia and Afghanistan and on into Pakistan, karez have been the principle source of both irrigation and drinking water within the living memory of today's inhabitants. In the late 1980s, Turkmenistan's minister of health told the Soviet press of his childhood in the Kopet Dag Mountains along the border with Iran: "In our small village in the desert, water came to us from the mountains via a system of karez, conceived and built by our forefathers, and the water was crystal clear and fresh. I still remember the taste." Since then, there has been rapid environmental decline. "The mountains were then covered with forests; now they are bald, and there is no water. The karez have crumbled and fallen in."

A few years ago, scientists at India's Centre for Water Resources Development and Management were amazed to discover more than 500 tunnels, locally called surangams, tapping water flowing off the Western Ghats in Kerala and irrigating coconut groves as far as the eye could see. It seems possible that this system was developed locally. Uncertainty also surrounds the origins of the qanat-like tunnels called *mambos* that irrigate paddy fields in Japan. Shoko Okazaki from the Persian Department of the Osaka University of Foreign Studies believes the technology reached Japan from Persia via China and Korea. Others think it may be indigenous.

One reason qanats have proved so successful over such a long period of time is that they are hydrologically self-regulating. They tap the underground water only up to the limit of natural replenishment. Unlike pumps, they cannot draw down the water table below the point at which they draw water. In practice, they restrict the flow to what is sustainable.

As a result, if properly designed and maintained, they yield water all year round—unlike many pumped boreholes and rivers. In Yemen, they are called the "unfailing springs." Their reliability has been a godsend during droughts, when qanats will often keep flowing as the land above dries out. But the downside is that you cannot turn them off. They flow constantly whether you need the water or not. Though in theory the tunnels could be fitted with watertight gates or drained into a large reservoir, this has rarely been done.

Not that qanats lack technical sophistication. Far from it. When the tunnels were very deep or the air underground bad, the excavators often dug two parallel tunnels so that they could quickly move from one to another to escape noxious fumes. To enable themselves to head in the right direction, the workers hung lanterns in the intermediate shafts. Lining the lamps up ensured that the tunnelers dug straight toward the mother well. Repairs were conducted using a wooden tripod erected above the well to lower the diggers and their tools. The skills displayed in using primitive spirit levels, rope, and candles were nonetheless sophisticated enough to allow the excavators to maintain steady gradients with a drop of 4 feet or less in every mile, in tunnels stretching for tens of miles. The equipment that Mitsis showed me one spring morning in the hills of Cyprus is identical to that used by generations of diggers from Persia to Oman, to China, to Morocco, to Pakistan.

Qanats, like many traditional water management technologies, are immensely laborious to build and maintain. A study in 1945 of one dig near Marrakesh in Morocco found that it took 6,000 person-days to dig a tunnel to irrigate 37 acres of fields, enough to feed just ten families. But the villagers had no choice if they wanted to eat. Digging and maintaining qanats was a huge undertaking even into the twentieth century in Persia, where the work has traditionally been carried out by a separate caste of well diggers, known as *mughani*. Mughani passed their skills on, in some secrecy, from father to son. In Yazd, where the mughanis were highly respected, it was said that even into the nineteenth century, one in seven of the working population was engaged in maintaining the qanat system. There was nothing more important in their societies than to secure water, and their entire social structure was framed to ensure that qanats were dug and maintained to meet that end.

Qanats seem to be suffering a cultural death at the very moment when their ecological virtues of sustainability and energy efficiency are being recognized. Nobody wants a return to the dreadful drudgery and danger that was the lot of qanat diggers of old. But can we find new forms of social ownership and organization that will allow the technologies, or modern variants of them, to revive? It is an important question to which we will return.

CHAPTER TWELVE

Common Monuments
to Human Perseverance

Europeans have always had their own visions of the wonders of the ancient world. Along with the pyramids of Egypt, the Colossus of Rhodes, and so on, they have always ranked the great feats of water engineering, such as the canals of Mesopotamia and the aqueducts of ancient Rome. And when exploring the rest of the world, Europeans have usually looked for similar edifices—Angkor Wat in Cambodia, for instance, or the great Inca city of Machu Pichu. But in revering such works, Europeans often missed the critical structures that maintained societies in many parts of the world. The imperial works were often mere adornments, baubles for the delight of kings and emperors, in comparison with the huge and often largely unremarked public works of irrigated agriculture. These are the real monuments to past civilizations in much of the world.

Perhaps the most spectacular of all these hydraulic works are the terraced hillsides of Asia. Terraces are the product of massive and highly organized human endeavor through the ages. These huge and sophisticated earthworks turn mountain slopes into towering "staircases" of narrow fields. Each step is held up by retaining walls and irrigated by water brought down the mountainside from springs or reservoirs, using a network of canals, sluices, and pipes. The terraces allow the hillside to be cultivated without all the soil washing away. They keep irrigation water on the fields. And, just as these terraces reengineer and fix the landscape on a large scale, they also fix the societies that run them. Villages to this day organize themselves into working groups that construct irrigation canals, terrace new slopes, plough the fields, and harvest the crops.

Among the most spectacular examples are the rice terraces that cover much of northern Luzon, the largest island in the Philippines. Often today dubbed the "eighth wonder of the world," they were among the few of these ancient works to gain modern recognition from archaeologists. Across the Cordillera highlands of Luzon, stone-walled terraces cling to mountainsides, rising between 2,000 and 5,000 feet above sea level. These giant stairways rise unbroken from riverbed to mountaintop at angles of up to 70 degrees. Each step is held in place by a dry-stone wall up to 30 feet high. The terraces are now UNESCO World Heritage Sites and have even become tourist destinations.

The first terraces of Luzon were built 3,000 or more years ago. The mountains were covered in terraces before the Romans built their aqueducts in Europe. And, unlike Roman waterworks, the terraces mostly remain in use, constantly maintained, extended, and improved by the descendants of the people who first built them. Despite centuries of tilling, the soils of the terraces remain as productive as ever. "Impeccable maintenance and the complex ecology of the ponded fields combine to make the subsistence systems stable, self-perpetuating, and nearly indestructible," says American anthropologist Charles Drucker.

The farmers developed strains of rice that can germinate in the cold conditions high up in these mountains. And their management of the local ecology is unsurpassed. Recently a giant worm invaded the terraces, apparently imported with new high-yield rice varieties from the International Rice Research Institute in southern Luzon. It caused massive erosion and threatened to undermine the terraces. Modern pesticides proved useless against it. But the Ifugao people who tend the terraces found the solution in an ancient method of pest control that involved treating the soil with a mulch made from vines from the surrounding forests.

■ Growing rice in hillside terraces is one of the most characteristic activities of the whole of Asia. According to British anthropologist and traveler John Reader, most of the continent's rice—by far the most important crop—is eaten within walking distance of where it is grown. The fecundity of this crop goes a long way to explaining the continent's high rural population. Certainly no other societies have proved capable of sustaining such dense populations in mountains areas for century after century. The reason is simple. Growing rice on irrigated terraces is labor-intensive work, requiring a large laboring population. But it is also highly productive. In the rich soils of islands such as Java and Bali, both in Indonesia, the rice terraces feed upwards of a 400 people per square mile.

But to achieve this level of productivity, farmers have evolved complex and, to many eyes, regimented social structures. The needs of the individual have to be subordinated to the communal will. On a terrace system, farmers cannot grow their rice when they want. Growing has to be staggered so as to share out the water most efficiently. Some terraces must be at the dry stage, whereas others require flooding. To break ranks would be disastrous. As Reader puts it: "People must work together in a very well organized and coordinated manner, building and maintaining terraces, ensuring adequate water flow, synchronizing the planting, and tending of the crops." The process is virtually self-perpetuating, he says. Confined to a limited patch of land, the culture turns in on itself. Practices become ritualized in religious and social behavior. "The threads run so tightly through all aspects of the society and culture that they have proved remarkably resistant to external attempts to pull them apart."

This history of the rice terraces of the Luzon Cordillera Mountains is intimately bound up with the Ifugao people, their religion and culture. Each stage in the farming cycle is accompanied by special religious ceremonies. The focal point of each village is a ritual rice field—the first to be planted and harvested. The owner of this field is traditionally in charge of the village granary and may also be the priest. He thus controls every aspect of the village's life.

In Bali, this social organization takes both secular and religious forms. In each village, there is a separate organization known as a *subak*, or "irrigation society," that determines who plants when. According to American anthropologist Clifford Geertz, there is one subak for each water source, whether a dam or a spring. Each branch of the distribution canal from that source also has its own neighborhood organization. Even the traditional Balinese year is 210 days long—precisely two growing seasons for a rice crop. And every move in the management of water and crops is written into the village religious calendar, drawn up at the island's famous water temples. Nestled among the reservoirs, irrigation canals, and rice terraces, the temples are ruled over by water priests, who are also the managers of the water and arbitrators of water and other disputes.

In essence, the rice terrace culture of Bali has been unchanged for more than a thousand years, absorbing first Hinduism from India and later Dutch colonial and Western cultures. Having to work so intensely together to feed themselves can turn individuals into mere cogs in a wheel, says Reader. Personal identity is lost, replaced by a profound fatalism. "People come and go, but the system persists."

That's a problem, of course, if the terraces are to continue. The sheer hard labor involved in maintaining and farming the terraces and irrigation channels has caused many to be abandoned all around the world. The steep terraces and narrow access paths mean that little farm machinery can reach these terraces. Everything from tilling to harvesting must be done by hand. Any traveler in the foothills of the Himalayas in northern India, for instance, will see vast swathes of abandoned terraces. The world's second most populous nation, with a billion people, suddenly seems depopulated.

Many people in the villages below buy food bought with money sent home by relatives working in the cities. And those who do work up in the mountain valleys are more likely to take laboring jobs making the numerous roads now being constructed through mountains than to till their terraces. Perhaps it is inevitable that as the social systems that sustained traditional terraced agricultural systems fail, so the systems themselves will fail. The stories of qanats and terraces seem remarkably similar in this respect. But can the world afford to lose the skills and insights that they contain? This is a critical issue that badly needs tackling if the hilly areas of the world are to remain productive.

■   Often these common monuments like agricultural terraces exist in the shadow of grander hydraulic works. Take Cambodia. Hundreds of thousands of people a year flock to Cambodia to see the great temples of Angkor. This huge urban conurbation, which flourished a thousand years ago, has been called "the Los Angeles of its time" and "the biggest city in the preindustrial era." It extended across some 500 square miles. And, like modern-day Los Angeles, it relied on a highly sophisticated system of hydraulic management that few tourists will so much as notice, even though several of its huge reservoirs, known as *barays*, and the channels that fed them from the Siem Reap River are still perfectly preserved and dotted in among the temples. Some barays still contain water. Locals still go bathing at the 5-mile-wide West Baray out near the airport and take boats to the temple on the island in the middle.

Many archaeologists have argued that without the reservoirs there would have been no temples. And yet there may be an even more interesting story, for the huge barays may not be the most significant elements in the Angkor water system. Recent mapping has shown that, aside from these large structures, a second, probably even larger network of waterworks existed to supply the villages and townships where most people in this suburban landscape carved from the rain forest lived and worked. Dozens of ponds have been uncovered. Some researchers argue that these are the true hydrological marvels of the Angkor civilization, for while the barays do not seem to have distributed their water anywhere, the ponds are connected by a sophisticated water distribution system to paddy fields that allowed the citizens of Angkor to harvest three and sometimes four crops of rice a year.

It was that rice that generated the wealth for the monarchs of Angkor, culminated in the building of the stupendous Angkor Wat temple in the twelfth century by King Suryavarman. The giant barays may, at best, have been only backup reservoirs for use during droughts when the village ponds failed. They could even have been purely ornamental—the baubles of kings to set beside their temples.

Much the same is probably true of the equally extraordinary hydrology of Sri Lanka, where at around the same time as Angkor was at its height, King Parakramabahu created another jungle city, Polonnaruwa. Today, the proud stone face of the king still looks out over the Sea of Parakrama, a man-made reservoir covering more than 10 square miles, one of many great reservoirs constructed during the civilization that once flourished there. Yet here too it turns out that these reservoirs may have been purely ceremonial or status symbols.

As at Angkor, in the shadow of the great structures was another network of smaller ponds and reservoirs that supplied the rice fields and villages of the kingdom. Every village had its rice paddy, and every paddy had its reservoir. As the late British anthropologist Edmund Leach commented: "When the central government was disrupted and the major works fell into disrepair, village life could carry on quite adequately." The wealth that supported the kings' ostentation came from more prosaic works—the forgotten hydrology of a rich civilization for whom the grand reservoirs were mere embellishments, perhaps paying homage to the real work of the villages.

■ There is a common pattern here. The world has been consistently blind to the importance to great empires of traditional communally managed water systems. Irrigated terraces from Peru to the Philippines, qanat networks across the Middle East and North Africa—plus the rainwater harvesting systems that we will look at shortly—all functioned as the hydraulic workhorses of glittering societies. Around the Mediterranean, we know about the great Roman water works. But here, too, there is a parallel, more humble but longer-lasting tradition.

Within a few hundred years of the close of the last ice age, the people living in the lands of present-day Syria, Lebanon, Israel, and Palestine founded one of the earliest, most stable, and most long lasting of all the farming systems on Earth. They were the first to cultivate wild grains, and by 6,000 years ago were growing olives and vines and figs. These societies were based on a more sustainable, more durable system of irrigation, tapping underground waters and catching the rains in ways that often persist to this day. Thousands of their water structures can be found in the deserts around the Mediterranean. They are just as useful as the great dams and structures of hydraulic civilizations, but they are rarely acknowledged by modern engineers because these structures don't form part of the lineage that engineers see as connecting their own endeavors to the great ancient waterworks. Yet in the twenty-first century, this other forgotten legacy may turn out to be much more useful to us.

Some of the most remarkable examples of this alternative hydraulic tradition have been found in the Negev Desert in Israel. Drive into the desert from Tel Aviv today and you can see how the Israelis use modern technology to make the desert margin bloom with water pumped south down the pipes of the National Water Carrier from the Sea of Galilee. Orange groves and greenhouses full of tomatoes dot the landscape. But if you drive farther, beyond the kibbutz farms and into the desert, where few modern farmers go, you slowly discover that early desert dwellers also made the desert green.

More than 1,500 years ago, the Negev Desert was inhabited by the Nabataeans, caravan traders who built six imposing desert cities. These included the famous and much visited "pink city" of Petra, close to the Jordan Valley, and farther west, Shivta and Avdat, along the spice road from the Mediterranean coast into the Middle East. These cities were models of how to live in the desert without the benefit of a river, water pipeline, or electric pump. Each of these hilltop cities is now in ruins. But the archaeological remains show that each has a complex network of gutters and drains. Some still feed virtually every drop of water landing within their walls into pools and cisterns sculpted from the rock. More intriguing still are the remains of oil and wine presses and wheat mills. How did the Nabataeans grow such crops in the desert, where rainfall is around 4 inches a year, most of it falling in a few short, sharp showers? Below the ramparts of Avdat, in the valley bottom, is the evidence: a series of stone-walled fields shining green in the desert.

Michael Evenari, an Israeli archaeologist from the Hebrew University in Jerusalem, excavated and renovated the Avdat farm and around a hundred other ancient farms in the Negev in the 1970s. When I visited the Avdat farm with his successor, Pedro Berliner, it hadn't seen rain for 6 weeks, but the soil was damp, a field of wheat was growing, almond trees were in leaf, and pistachio trees would soon follow. The miracle had been achieved by six lines of stone walls, each about 18 inches high, winding from a nearby hill to the farm. The walls captured the occasional flash floods high on the slopes and brought the water down to the fields below.

As I explored this remarkable farm, Israel was facing a water crisis. The Israeli Water Commission had warned orchard owners to expect heavy price increases for water, plus a 70 percent cut in supply. "Until now," said Berliner, "our pistachio nuts from this farm have not been economically viable. But as water prices rise for modern farms out here in the desert, this kind of runoff farming is going to look increasingly attractive."

Once someone shows you the stone walls in the Negev, you spot them everywhere. The desert is marked by long lines of rocks hugging the contours and spanning wadis. Some once funneled water to farms. Some still do, ensuring that, even in the driest years, small patches of green survive as emergency pasture for the Bedouin herds. Other lines of walls fill cisterns—caverns dug into the chalk hillsides to provide drinking water for sheep and goats and their Bedouin shepherds. The cisterns were the basis of survival for the Bedouin a thousand years before the Nabataeans built their cities. And they still are. As one Israeli academic who has studied them told me: "There are no drinking water problems in the Negev—if you know where to look."

■   All across North Africa—in Morocco and Algeria, Tunisia and the Sinai region of Egypt—such technologies have been critical in allowing survival in the desert for millennia. Cross the Sahara Desert and the same technologies can be seen to the south. The Hausa people in Niger and the Mossi of Burkina Faso, the inhabitants of the Ouaddai area of Chad, and the Hiraan region of Somalia all use similar techniques. Two millennia ago, Libyans turned what today is desert land far from the coast into the granary of the Roman Empire. Watered with the occasional rains, suitably harvested, and distributed across the land, the fields produced wheat and barley, olives and grapes, figs and dates. "There is," says Dieter Prinz of the University of Karsruhe in Germany, "no evidence of climatic change since the Roman period." All that is different is the ability of local farmers to harness the elements. In the intervening years, Libyans have clearly forgotten more than they have learned. As British archaeologist and water expert David Gilbertson puts it: "The frequency of ancient settlements in the arid lands of North Africa and Arabia suggests that the wisdom of the ancients in managing these harsh landscapes was more substantive than our own."

As water crises become increasingly common in this century, we may be forced to rediscover the value of that wisdom. Yet water management is increasingly tied to the construction of large dams and diversions, and the ancient knowledge and traditional cultural systems of water management may well disappear. Modern civil engineers may count this as a small price to pay for the ability to meet the water needs of the world's dramatically increased populations. Closer examination, however, reveals that these systems often worked on scales and at levels of efficiency unimagined by most of us in the West.

CHAPTER THIRTEEN

America's Lost Hydraulic Civilizations

"The entire region is hopeless desert. It is unadapted for agriculture." So wrote Captain David DuBose Gaillard, a military engineer sent out to survey the Sonoran Desert on the Arizona border with Mexico in 1894. Yet, barren as it appeared, he noted that there were everywhere secret water holes known only to the Papago Indians, who had occupied the desert for thousands of years. The Papago also had a mysterious system for farming in the desert. "When the July rains commence, the Papago forsake their ranches and hasten to their fields, where they plant corn, pumpkins, melons, etc.," he wrote.

Gaillard, who a decade later became famous as an engineer on the Panama Canal, was in awe. Many other travelers through these arid lands, among them legions of would-be gold miners, had dismissed the Papago as mere nomads, eating wild food like saguaro fruit, mesquite bean pods, and cholla cactus flower buds. The visitors tended to see what they wanted to see—a wild, untamed landscape, an empty canvas for their own heroic exploits. They had no wish to acknowledge inhabitants whose ability to live in the hostile environment was, as Gaillard realized, markedly superior to their own.

Gaillard was a busy military man, but he stayed long enough to write a treatise on the Papago for the *American Anthropologist*. He noted how they switched from gathering wild foods and raising cattle and horses to farming whenever rain could be coaxed into watering their lands. But he did not investigate their methods, and the popular view of the Papago did not improve. By early in the twentieth century, the European invaders— whose military superiority, at least, was unquestioned—had penned the Papago within the 9,000-acre San Xavier Reservation, southwest of Tucson. Yet where they could access tillable land, the Papago could still farm in a manner that no European could emulate, husbanding the scarce rains to grow crops. How did they do it?

The first written record of the Papago's methods of irrigation do not appear until 1917, when H. V. Clotts of the U.S. Indian Services wrote that "they have a very ingenious plan of throwing long dikes or wings, which converge on a few acres like the sides of a funnel. Thus the rainfall from hundreds of acres is diverted into a pocket of a few acres, where the soil is suitable for cultivation." The Papago, who changed their name in the 1980s to the Tohono O'Odham, or "desert people," carried out one of the oldest arts of water management—rainwater harvesting. To do it, they constructed mile after mile of low embankments across the desert. Some, like the Nabataeans in the Negev Desert in Israel, concentrated the occasional floodwaters coming off the desert into irrigation channels. Others, like the spate irrigators of Yemen, captured stormwater flowing down mountain wadis and spread it across fields.

Much later in 1954, the leading American economic botanist, Edgar Anderson, described the desert agriculture of the Papago as "one of the most remarkable agricultural systems in the world." But by then the embankments were all derelict, the former fields either abandoned or dotted with houses, schools, and chapels. And many of the water channels had dried up or turned to concrete to supply cities.

More recently, the intimate relationship between the Papago, the Sonoran Desert, and its rains has been described in greater, and more eloquent, detail by Gary Paul Nabhan. A Lebanese American ethnobotanist, Nabhan has for more than 20 years devoted his life to preserving traditional seeds and crops in the American West, first as an academic at the University of Arizona and later running his own nonprofit organization. He has identified in much greater detail than his predecessors the different structures used by the Papago to catch the rains. They included brush weirs that spread the floodwaters and gravity-fed channels, called *arroyos,* that lead the water from diversion weirs made of earth or sticks. Elsewhere, if the supply of brush gave out, the Papago switched to constructing bunds made of rocks. From the Chaco Canyon in New Mexico to the hills around Tucson and Phoenix in Arizona, the remains of these structures are there for anyone who knows where and how to look.

In recent years, deep wells have been sunk into a fast-disappearing aquifer beneath the Sonoran Desert to allow the Papago once again to irrigate a few fields—mostly, these days, of cotton. And, in anticipation of the aquifer's running out, the authorities have allocated large amounts of water from the Central Arizona Project. This $4 billion piece of modern engineering brings water by canal from the distant Colorado River to Phoenix and Tucson. But it is hardly a triumph of modernity to first force the Papago to give up harvesting rainwater on their own land, then spend billions of dollars bringing them water that fell as snow hundreds of miles away on the mountains of Colorado and Wyoming.

■ Some vestiges of the old ways remain. In the far north of Arizona, the Hopi Indians still cultivate fertile valley soils, which they created for themselves long ago by building low stone walls to capture the water and silt rushing from gullies in the surrounding hills. But all across the American West, modern, hugely expensive water distribution systems have been built on top of the remains of once-flourishing agricultural civilizations, many of which used local water with far greater sophistication than we can muster today. To the south of the Hopi lands, the sprawling desert metropolis of Phoenix is built on the remains of extensive irrigation canals dug by the Hohokam Nation, who diverted the waters of the Salt River to irrigate their fields. The Hohokam irrigation system, which also harnessed waters from the Gila and Verde Rivers, was probably the most extensive irrigation system north of Mexico. Construction continued over almost a millennium, from AD 300 to the arrival of Europeans on the continent. Eventually the canals extended more than 600 miles. These civilizations are mostly gone, but the question remains whether it is beyond us to relearn the lessons of the ancients.

When Columbus first set foot on its shore, the New World had nearly one-third of the world's population. Many centers of population supported more people than they do today. South America in particular has yet to recapture the agricultural productivity it enjoyed before the Europeans arrived. This is largely because the inhabitants have lost the pre-Columbian skills in managing water. In the Andes, the Incas and others had created magnificent systems of irrigated terraces that covered more than 2 million acres of steep, often near-vertical mountainsides in Peru. Today, more than half of the terraces are abandoned. Their decline has mirrored the decline in Peru as a whole, as the hills are depopulated and millions have moved, in poverty, to the capital, Lima. The Chimu Empire, in the country's northern coastal desert, constructed hundreds of irrigation canals, aqueducts, and tunnels very similar to the qanats of the Old World to bring water from the glacial rivers of the Andes.

Archaeologists have rightly praised the prowess of the South American empires that left behind great monuments such as the Chimu headquarters at Chan-Chan and the Incas' first city of Macchu Picchu. But until recently they have missed the even larger earthworks that transformed the South American grasslands, or *pampas*, into farms that sustained a sizable portion of the Americas' estimated hundred million inhabitants. And there is tantalizing evidence emerging that these grassland civilizations extended deep into what is today the Amazon rain forest.

These earthworks took the form of corrugated fields. Abandoned after the arrival of the Europeans, they remained invisible to outsiders for almost five centuries. They were only rediscovered in the 1950s, when oil prospectors drove their swamp buggies out across the Llanos de Mojos in remote northeastern Bolivia, an area of grassy lowland across which several Amazon tributaries flood each year. The prospectors had an unexpectedly bumpy ride. What they thought was a flat plain turned out to be an endless landscape of shallow ridges, each no more than a yard high. The network of ridges covered around 100 square miles.

Subsequent research has shown that indigenous peoples painstakingly dug these ridges a thousand or more years ago. It must have been one of the most large-scale pieces of landscape gardening ever attempted. The raised ridges created dry soils in which crops would grow while the rest of the plain was flooded. They seem to have been highly productive. Several hundred thousand people probably once lived on this land. Among the ridges, and raised a bit higher, are a thousand miles of causeways and what could be burial mounds and villages. But today the fields, canals, causeways, dikes, and artificial lakes are abandoned and forgotten by the locals. And the land now has many times more cattle than people.

Like the desert walls of the Negev, once you know how to look, raised fields turn up everywhere, says Clark Erickson of the University of Pennsylvania, who has spent several years painstakingly uncovering them. In northern Colombia, there is a flat, low-lying basin near the town of San Marcos that floods half the year. "When the waters retreat, the grass appears as stripes for several weeks, with the ridges brown and the ditches bright green," he says. In Ecuador, you can see ridges across the river from Guayaquil International Airport. There are more along the coastline of Surinam. Small versions have been found in North America in Michigan and Wisconsin. But the most intensively studied raised fields lie on the shores of Lake Titicaca, high in the cold Altiplano of southern Peru.

To the modern eye, the Altiplano is poor farming land. The soils are heavy and waterlogged on the flat plains, and thin and poor on the slopes. Killing frosts, severe droughts, and heavy floods are frequent. Crops don't grow well. Yet, historically, this was no desert. It is where the potato was first cultivated. And sometime about 3,000 years ago, lakeside communities of Quecha Indians began digging long ditches and piling the earth into ridges across a plain ten times the size of Manhattan.

Erickson thought he would try to do what Evenari did with the stone walls of the Negev Desert and re-create the ancient farming system on the shores of Lake Titicaca. But he could go one better than Evenari. For, unlike the Nabateans, the Quecha, whose ancestors dug the first ridges, were still around. The current residents of the area revered their ancestors and believed they had been left behind by a "first race" who ruled the area long ago. At the beginning of the 1980s, when Erickson proposed reviving the ridge system, a group of Quecha villagers agreed to take part in the experiment. Under his supervision, they dug a series of ridges and ditches across the Titicaca marshes, using traditional tools.

By 1990, they had drained more than 250 acres of marsh and created ridges that they planted with traditional Andean potatoes and grains. The results were spectacular. The fields raised crops clear of ground frosts, kept salt at bay, and created fertilizer each summer in the form of algae-filled mud from the ditches. These ancient systems of water management have proved dramatically superior to anything else in use in the region today. During drought, the ridged fields of Lake Titicaca have produced crops when nearby, conventionally farmed crops have failed. When flooding inundated neighboring fields, the ridges kept plants dry. And in more typical years, yields of potatoes are three times the yield of nearby farms. As a bonus, the farmers have found that the ditches attract fish and birds for the pot.

So successful was Erickson's experiment that local churches and political parties soon included raised fields in their aid projects. One party constructed a large block of fields in the shape of its logo. More substantially, British archaeologist Anne Kendall has formed a trust fund to re-create ancient Peruvian water and agriculture systems by building water channels to abandoned terraces and raised fields.

Erickson says there is huge scope to relearn the lessons of the past and adopt ancient technologies of water management across South America. Yields on his Peruvian farms could theoretically allow 1.5 million people to live and feed themselves in the Lake Titicaca basin, several times the current population. The revival of raised fields could provide farmers all over the region with a good living growing cash crops as well as staple foods—this in an area where several ambitious projects to import Western farming methods have failed.

■   In one place in Latin America, the ancient systems of managing the landscape and its water have continued in operation without a break to the present day. Bizarrely, this has happened in the suburbs of Mexico City, the second-largest metropolis in the world. Its squatter slums sprawl across the dried-up beds of a series of lakes that once filled the Valley of Mexico. But the remnants of a few lakes survive. The largest is Lake Xochimilco, home to the city's last *chinampas,* or "floating gardens," an ancient system of farming that remains one of the most productive in the Western Hemisphere. "Floating gardens" is a bit of a misnomer since they are firmly attached to the lake bottom. The gardens, in fact, comprise a thick sandwich of succeeding layers of mud and vegetation in the midst of the lake.

Two thousand years ago the chinampas of the Valley of Mexico fed the vast pyramid city of Teotihuacán. Around 1,500 years later they fed the Aztec Empire at a time when its capital, Tenochtitlán, was perhaps the largest city in the world, as big as Seville or Córdoba in Spain. When the conquistador Hernán Cortés arrived in Mexico in 1519, he described the Aztec capital as another Venice, a city with tens of thousands of canoes traversing myriad canals and a series of shallow lakes. Surrounding it, he said, were tens of thousands of "tillers who dwelt in the middle of swamps." Called *chinamperos,* these tillers had turned the lakes into a patchwork of raised fields, each about 100 yards long and 10 yards wide, surrounded by waterways.

Recent archaeological evidence suggests that the chinampas covered wide areas of the Valley of Mexico. But today, after centuries of draining, the lakes within Mexico City itself are mostly gone, and as their dried-out beds shrink, the entire city is sinking. The remains of the main Aztec city lake, Texcoco, is a fetid pond between the city's largest squatter colony and its international airport. But in the southern suburbs, beside the new city of Xochimilco, the lake of the same name survives. Though only a sixth of its former size, it continues to produce fruit, vegetables, and flowers.

These days the area is a welcome picnic spot for tourists and city-dwellers alike to sniff the beds of gardenias, hibiscus, and roses. But to keep the gardens fertile, the modern-day chinamperos still follow the tradition of many centuries, paddling down the waterways in narrow, flat-bottomed boats before each planting season to scoop mud from the lake bottom onto the gardens with buckets attached to long poles. Modern pollution has killed the fish that used to swim in the canals, but the surviving 500 acres of chinampas are hugely fertile. The gardens remain a flourishing testimony to how the valley's great civilizations once fed themselves. They may be among the longest continually cultivated areas on the planet.

CHAPTER FOURTEEN

How to Catch the Rain

Across the Indian state of Gujarat, the farmers are waiting. As water tables plummet, their pumps fail, and their fields dry up, they are waiting for the sound of a new source of water: the gurgling sound of water coming from a dam to the south on the River Narmada. They have been promised the water for years. Some of the canals that will deliver it have been dug for many years. Occasionally a little water comes—usually just before a local election.

Politicians know how crucial water is to survival and prosperity in India. The promise of more water is a regular mantra of the political debate in a country where farmers make up most of the population. It is not for nothing known as the land of a million villages. And for two decades now, dams on the sacred River Narmada have been held out to Gujarat's farmers as the ultimate solution to their problems. But regular supplies at the critical time of the season when they need it? No. After a decade, many are growing weary of the promises of the state engineers. Even if the water is there—and the great Sardar Sarovar Dam on the Narmada River is undoubtedly filling, as the 80,000 people who are being forced to make way for it will attest—there is no guarantee that it will ever reach intended beneficiaries, the poor farmers of Gujarat.

But now there is new talk in the barren fields of Gujarat, which is one of India's most arid states. They don't have to wait for the state to deliver water that may never come. They can catch their own. Catch the monsoon rains, says the new word in the villages, and you will never go short.

One man who has done it is Haradevsinh Hadeja, a cricket-playing former police officer. He has remade his village in the backwoods of southern Gujarat so that it can capture the monsoon rains and keep them to fill taps, irrigate crops, and even beautify the village with trees and ponds. Just off the main road to the town of Rajkot, where Mahatma Gandhi went to school, the village of Rajsamadhiya is a revelation in this parched landscape of dying rivers, empty wells, occasional visits from emergency water tankers, and the long, long wait for Narmada water.

Hadeja's is no overnight success. He began work 25 years ago, trying to catch the rain. "I am an uneducated person. I saw that people were leaving the village, and I wanted to develop the village so they could stay. That meant growing more crops, which meant finding more water," he told me as we toured the village. He had noticed how many villages in the area still had traditions of collecting water in ponds that kept going through the nine-month dry season. They provided a little water for cattle and an emergency source of water for the villages. He simply developed that idea, he says. He surveyed the land in his own village and found eight low-lying areas into which the monsoon rain naturally flowed. "We decided to channel more water into those low areas. We built dykes to channel the flow and small dams to keep the water once it had arrived."

He soon found that much of the water in the new ponds soon disappeared below ground into the sandy soil. Disaster? It turned out not. For this water did not travel far, and it soon began to fill the village's wells. While other villages were finding that their wells were going dry, in

Rajsamadhiva the water table was rising, and dried-up wells were returning to life. The ponds found their real worth in refilling the village wells.
The village was becoming an oasis in a growing desert.

Word spread about his endeavors. "After 1994, I began to meet scientists who came here to see what we were doing and to offer their own
expertise," he says. One group of scientists turned up with satellite images
of the village that helped him refine the drainage system. He identified
hidden cracks in the geology below the village that drained rainwater
away before it had a chance to fill wells and nourish the soil. By plugging
them with concrete, he kept more water for the village. Today, the water
table through the village is just 20 feet from the surface, compared with
typically 100 feet in surrounding villages.

"Most of the villages around here don't have enough water. They are
growing dependent on water tankers coming to give them drinking water.
But even in dry years we have enough water here," says Jaivir Singh, vice
president of the Rajsamadhiya village council. "Since 1978 not a single
government water tanker has entered this village. We have more than
doubled the amount of water available in the village. We are growing three
crops sometimes where we had one before. On my land, I grow groundnuts and wheat and vegetables where my father only grazed a few cattle.
Prosperity is growing among the people."

Prosperity is relative, of course. As he spoke, a team of lower-caste
women were breaking stones in the hot sun outside the room where we
met. But you could see that anywhere in India. And a tour of this village
of 1,700 people was a revelation. The heart of the village—a Hindu community with a preponderance of people from the Patel caste—appears
conventional enough, a gaggle of rough stone-built single-story buildings
along a series of tracks leading from the small square where the small

village hall is situated. But beyond the village center, among the small fields planted with wheat and vegetables and cotton and groundnuts, it is quickly obvious that the landscape is greener than in most Gujarati villages. There are thousands of fruit trees, whereas many villages are treeless. There is shade as you walk, and piles of mangoes and watermelons everywhere besides the paths. Cactuses remind you that this is a naturally arid landscape, but they are used as field borders to keep out livestock. And most noticeable, there are many water ponds between the fields, whereas other villages are dry. Admiring the blues and greens, I suddenly heard a mobile phone ringing in the field. Hadeja grins. "Ecological wealth is bringing financial wealth to the village, too," he says. "My father grazed cattle, but I have turned the pasture to growing tomatoes, groundnuts, cotton, and wheat. My father's income from his farm was two lakhs a year [200,000 rupees, or around $4,500]. I earn ten lakhs from the same property. I have a car and everything."

Altogether, there are forty-five water collecting structures in the village. Many of them are arranged in lines along drainage routes. Thus water seeping from one pond finds its way into the next and so on. I watched women washing clothes beside a percolation pond that collects water flowing off the land up to 3 miles away. The purpose is always to hold water on the land so that it can recharge the underground reserves and fill the wells. At the highest point in the village Hadeja has even removed the topsoil. Surely, it makes no sense to remove such a precious commodity as soil, I asked. But Hadeja insists that the removal makes sense because it increases the rate of infiltration of water into the subsoil. Amid the water, there are trees everywhere. More than 60,000 are in the 2 square miles within the village limits. And with trees there is shade, and a better microclimate.

The village has rules about how the water can be used. The most striking is that there should be no pumping water out of the ponds. They are there purely now to refill the village's wells. Farmers get their water that way only. The village council also bans the introduction of water-intensive crops like sugarcane. Farmers can grow cash crops, but only the less water-intensive ones like wheat and groundnuts. There is no point in catching more water if it is only wasted on water-thirsty crops, said Hadeja.

Rajsamadhiya is one of the most sophisticated examples of a village using rainwater harvesting in India. But other villages are also developing similar techniques, and some are getting remarkable results. In a village called Limbadia, in Bhavnagar District in Gujarat, a series of small check-dams built to hold up the flow of water in a small stream created artesian conditions in nearby wells. Wells dug to 150 feet that before had been dry suddenly began gushing water during the monsoon season. And even during the dry season the village water table was just 8 feet below the surface.

Scientists are beginning to take notice too. Among them is Tushaar Shah, who runs a groundwater research unit at the Sri Lankan–based International Water Management Institute, which has set up a base in Gujarat partly to learn the lessons of places like Rajsamadhiya. Nobody has managed to develop such a complete system as Hadeja, Shah says. "It's the model for what everyone else is trying to do. And it certainly beats waiting for the Narmada water."

■ India has a long tradition of harvesting the rains, of course. It was the dominant method of water collection before the arrival of British imperial engineers. Arthur Cotton, the British Empire's legendary irrigation engineer, spoke in old age about his admiration of "the multitude of old [water]works in India which show boldness and engineering talent and have stood for hundreds of years." He was referring in the main to the country's tanks, the shallow mud-walled reservoirs constructed over the centuries in valley bottoms to capture the monsoon rains. Around Chennai, formerly Madras, where Cotton was based for much of his career, he found more than 50,000 such tanks, around a third of them privately built and owned, and the rest in public use.

Before the arrival of the British, tank construction was a major activity in millions of villages, with local chiefs organizing construction in return for the support of religious and caste leaders. But the decline of feudal land-tenure systems often destroyed the social ties that built and maintained tanks, after which many became silted up and abandoned. Other states, particularly in the hot south, are also festooned with tanks. The small state of Karnataka has 35,000 village tanks, for instance. Tamil Nadu has 39,0000, irrigating around 2.5 million acres. Taken together, they total several percent of the land surface of India. Archaeologists have since uncovered sophisticated brick-lined tanks dating back 2,700 years. Most tanks were small, covering a couple of acres or so and irrigating perhaps 50 acres of paddy while also replenishing local wells. But often the patchwork of small village tanks and irrigation systems was overlain by a network of larger reservoirs that probably fed imperial cities, armies, and parks. The largest covered 40 square miles and had more than 10 miles of embankments around them.

Many Gandhian groups have adopted the technology in recent years. In the southern state of Karnataka, on the high arid plains west of Bangalore, I toured areas where they have created landscapes of hundreds of interconnecting farm ponds (similar to the tanks discussed above), arranged in scientifically designed chains to augment the underground waters. At Adihalli, near the town of Tiptur, three hundred farm ponds have transformed the farming potential of a series of villages. As a rule of thumb, these systems devote 1 percent of the land to ponds.

Villagers growing coconuts and chilies, coffee and cashews, vegetables and gherkins and rice attested to the new fertility of the land. I even met goat herders who had traveled several miles to find pasture for their animals close to a village pond. "Where we live there is no water," they told me. "As the ponds around dry up, more and more people come here for water." In one village, farmers said the ponds had raised the water table by more than 200 feet. Farmers who had become migrant laborers because their own land was barren have returned to grow crops once more.

■ The idea has also been taken up by Hindu religious groups. The most notable is Swadhyaya Pariwar, whose leader, Pandurang Shastri Athavale, a vedic scholar based in southern Gujarat, began to inspire his followers in the late 1980s to catch the monsoon rains. Dada, as his followers called him, died in October 2003, at age 84. He preached a simple reflective and virtuous life, but one that stressed the creation of a wholesome community in which the value of commonly owned resources such as water are revered and their protection is regarded as an act of devotion to God. In coastal areas, his followers have set up communal fishing boats that distribute fish to the poor, and in the arid farms of Gujarat, they have pioneered communal efforts in villages to improve the water supply, especially by catching the rains. Dada got his ideas for collecting rainwater after going to Israel and seeing the rainwater harvesting structures of the Nabateans that had been unearthed by archaeologists such as Evenari in the 1970s. Dada incorporated the idea into a green philosophy of communal management of natural resources. His acolytes went out into the fields of Gujarat to preach the new ecological gospel of capturing the rains.

Farmers who had until then sought to get rid of monsoon floodwaters by diverting them onto the fields of their neighbors began instead to catch the rain in ponds to recharge their wells. In many cases, they did not stop at digging ponds to allow water to infiltrate into the underground waters. They also installed pipes to send the water directly from the ponds down their own wells. Others sank boreholes into the bottom of ponds to speed recharge of the aquifer. One farmer in Gondal District said he initially didn't understand the teachings of Dada. "But we thought that if Dada says we should do it, then that is what we will do." It proved so successful that "village people kept telling me that Dada had brought Narmada to my field."

There are few detailed records of how widely these ideas have been followed, says Shah. But he estimates that thousands of new ponds have been dug and tens or even hundreds of thousands of wells have benefited. Shah calls it "new natural resource ethic . . . mobilizing social energy on such a scale and intensity that may be one of the most effective responses to an environmental challenge anywhere in the world." It is, he says, "completely autonomous from government. It emerged on its own, found its own source of energy and dynamism, and devised its own expansion plans." Could government adopt it? On the whole, he thought not. "Propagating only the techniques without their ethical foundation may be of little value, and if the movement sustains itself and spreads only on the basis of its narrow technical and economic rationale, this precious capital will probably be lost. At the very least, government should avoid harming the movement by misconceived subsidy programs."

Shah believes that only a strong social movement, backed by a figure like Dada, could achieve such benefits. No individualist ethic based on personal profit could do it. "If only one or two people carry out recharge in a village, then the benefits will be shared too thinly. But if a whole village does, then the benefits are greater and shared by all. That is when you see a real difference." Dada put it another way: "If you quench Mother Earth's thirst, she will quench yours."

■   The danger lurking behind the successes of movements like the one Dada inspired is that it risks breeding the myth that harvesting the rain somehow creates more water. That is not necessarily so. The problem is that whenever you catch the rain as it falls and store it in tanks or direct it into underground reserves, there will be less water flowing into rivers. And whenever river basins reach the point where virtually no water is leaving the catchment, where every last drop is corralled and diverted and utilized, then every drop captured by an upstream rainwater harvester will be lost to a downstream user. This is already the case in parts of India, for instance, where rainwater harvesting is being adopted by farmers and local authorities with greater vigor.

That's what the critics of rainwater harvesting say, anyway. And they have a point. But Shah says this should not be taken as an automatic argument against rainwater harvesting. Far from it. He accepts that "planners must look at rainwater harvesting on the river basin perspective. In a closed basin, such as many in India, any significant modification in one part of the system will certainly adversely affect people in other parts."

But, he says, the equation is not so straightforward. Rainwater harvesters usually use their water more efficiently than the recipients of water from downstream state irrigation schemes. Big downstream reservoirs usually have large surface areas from which evaporation may remove up to a fifth of the water so expensively captured. Community-organized rainwater harvesting will often serve poor farmers better than centrally run state irrigation projects. And, by avoiding all manner of expensive concrete pouring and pump installation, it is also likely to be far cheaper.

There are also what Shah calls "socioecological gains." Rainwater collected in ponds and tanks and allowed to seep into soils and underground aquifers serves many purposes besides simple water supply for irrigation. It provides local habitat for fish, water for livestock and trees, and protection against floods and accompanying soil erosion; it maintains high water tables that keep wells from drying up and leaves silt for fertilizing fields on the bottoms of the tanks.

In an increasing number of river basins, it is impossible to argue that rainwater harvesting is collecting "new" water, says Shah. But it is right to argue that it is making better use of the water. Both the water efficiency and rainwater harvesting innovations make eminent sense for individual farmers. But problems arise if simple-minded water managers start assuming that every drop of water "saved" through more efficient on-farm irrigation or "captured" through new rainwater harvesting structures is a net gain of water that can be used to irrigate more crops or fill more taps. It just isn't so.

■   The competing claims of Dada and the Narmada engineers to water the fields of Gujarat make a telling vignette of a battle being fought out across the developing world. It is between those who believe that Western-style water delivery systems will solve the problems of poor farmers and rural communities, and those who believe in an entirely different strategy of small, ecologically friendly systems, based often on traditional methods of water management.

All across India, such contrasts between large-scale and small-scale engineering for water can be seen. In Rajasthan two decades ago, the

Indian government built at huge cost the Indira Ghandi Canal. It snakes for 450 miles through the Thar Desert close to the border with Pakistan. It has a clear political purpose—to populate with Indians a desert region that is the frequent source of border disputes between the two countries. And it ostentatiously uses India's "share" of the River Indus, from which the canal is supplied. But in agricultural terms it has proved a failure. The canal area is not populated by happy, prosperous farmers. Many of the fields are waterlogged. The side channels from the canals fill with weeds, and the fields shine with deposits of salt—the inevitable result of over-irrigation. Mosquitoes breed in the stagnant canal water. A major malaria epidemic in 2003 left hundreds dead.

In Rajasthan, the real gains in farming are mostly coming, as in Gujarat, from harvesting the rains. Across the state, villagers are digging *johads*, the local name for ponds that collect runoff from the surrounding area. The guru for the movement in Rajasthan is Rajendhra Singh, a government scientist who taught himself traditional water management skills and went out to the villages with the aim of turning back the Thar Desert, which was advancing across the state. "I saw village after village emptying because of water shortages," he says. His movement in Rajasthan now has 45 full-time staff and funding from the Ford Foundation. It claims responsibility for helping build some 4,500 water-harvesting structures. In places, he has proved so successful at reviving local underground water reserves through allowing more water to soak underground that the water table has reached the surface, and rivers have started to flow where none flowed before. Two rivers, the Ruparel and Arvari, have returned to the map, thanks to Singh's work.

While the man-made canals intended to bring water from the Narmada Dam in Gujarat still remain resolutely dry in spite of a decade of promises from politicians and engineers, a nudge to nature by helping villagers to refill natural aquifers has ensured that natural water channels are now running. Indians hearing stories about the politicians' latest plans to construct a national water grid by spending tens of billions of dollars to link up rivers may draw the obvious lesson.

CHAPTER FIFTEEN

The People's Green Revolution

Jane Ngei is a 30-year-old Kenyan mother and farmer. She built her own dam with an ox-plough, a spade, and a wheelbarrow. It is not a big dam. It is less than 50 feet across. "It collects the water running down the road after it rains," she told me. But it is enough to irrigate her dozen or so acres of maize, vegetables, and fruit trees, and to keep her small herd of cattle and goats from going thirsty. Ngei's six head of cattle, fed on the fodder crops she grows on her land, contribute manure for her fields as well as milk that she sells to a dairy in nearby Masii town. None of this would be possible without the dam.

Jane's is hardly the kind of dam to turn back the tide of history, you might think. And yet according to conventional environmental wisdom, Ngei's farm and hundreds of others throughout the drought-prone hills of Machakos, east of Nairobi, should not be here. This landscape should long since have turned to dust and blown away. Sixty years ago, a British colonial soil inspector by the name of Colin Mather condemned these hills as "an appalling example" of environmental degradation in which "the inhabitants are rapidly drifting to a state of hopeless and miserable poverty, and their land to a parched desert of rocks, stones and sand."

Much the same was said in the 1950s and again in the 1970s. And throughout this period, with Kenya recording the fastest population growth rate of any country in the world, the population of Machakos rose a staggering fivefold.

The Akamba people first came to the area during the seventeenth and eighteenth centuries. They did a little cultivation but mainly raised livestock and traded. When the Europeans arrived in the late nineteenth century, the Akamba seemed to get on well with them, signing treaties with the British, welcoming missionaries, and doing deals with the British East Africa Company. For a while, before the capital moved to Nairobi, Machakos was the seat of the British Protectorate of East Africa. But in 1906, the British penned the Akamba into a "native reserve," and it may have been around then that pressure of grazing increasingly large herds of livestock on the hills of Machakos began to push the area toward desertification—pressure that grew as the twentieth century progressed.

A recipe for disaster, surely? And yet these hills have failed to turn to desert. Today, they are greener and more heavily planted with trees, more productive and less eroded than at any time during the twentieth century. What went right? The "Machakos miracle" has excited interest because of claims that rising population was the best thing that happened. It forced the farmers to change from cattle herding to settled farming. It gave them the laborers to work the land properly, and in particular to husband its fickle water resources. Whatever the truth of the population argument, it is undeniable that sophisticated management of the region's water has been at the heart of its revival and may hold a powerful lesson for others.

The techniques adopted by the Machakos farmers are far from uniform. Ngei is one of hundreds of farmers in these hills, the heartland of the Akamba people, who have dug small dams to catch the rains. She irrigates her crops by siphoning water from her tiny reservoir into a simple bucket attached to a perforated hose. Others have planted trees to keep moisture in the soils or constructed terraces up the steep hillsides to trap rainfall and prevent soil from washing away. Many farmers use a technique known locally as *fanya-juu* terracing, which involves digging a ditch and throwing the soil upslope to form an earth wall that holds rain on the land. Either way, the methods are simple and can be done on a small scale with little communal organization—self-help farmers' organizations and women's groups (since women are the main farmers) form gangs to work on one another's farms when needed. By refusing to bow to the inevitable, the Akamba farmers have offered a challenge to the doomsayers of desertification and the harbingers of a hydrological Armageddon.

■ The Akamba farmers, it turns out, first saw many of these water structures while serving with British colonial forces in India during the Second World War. They decided to try the same thing when they got home, combining water management with a variety of new crops. What was once a subsistence economy, geared to nothing more than short-term survival on crumbling soils, has turned into something much more productive and environmentally sustainable.

Such cross-fertilization of ideas has, as we have seen, played a big part in the spread of rainwater harvesting ideas around the developing world. Indian religious leaders got the idea from seeing the Nabataean structures uncovered by archaeologists in Israel. And that source also helped turn around farming in West Africa, thanks to an observant Oxfam worker. Bill Hereford was a local field director in Burkina Faso in the late 1970s. But during that time he spent a year's sabbatical in Israel, during which he looked at how Evenari and his colleagues had successfully replicated the

Nabataean structures at Avdat. If it can be done in the Negev Desert, he wondered, why not in Burkina Faso?

His inspiration came just in time. Drought was stripping the vegetation from the fields of Burkina Faso's Yatenga Province, where he worked. The soil was forming a crust that the occasional rains could not penetrate. Local farmers had no answer to their plight. The European Development Fund had stepped in twice to help. The first time, its workers drove bulldozers across the land to create earth dykes in hopes of the rain on the fields, but the fields became waterlogged. Then the workers drilled hundreds of wells, but the water table sank and the wells dried up. Meanwhile the local acacia trees, one of the last and hardiest barriers to the desert, succumbed to the drought. It looked like the Sahara was taking over.

But Hereford began to suggest a radical new approach to local farmers. He proposed a last effort to keep water on their land and prevent terminal soil erosion. Why not, he said, collect up the large number of stones that littered the landscape and use them to make low stone walls along the contour lines of the hillsides. The stones would both stop the occasional heavy rains from washing away the soils and hold on to the water itself long enough for it to penetrate the soil and reach the roots of plants.

The first farmer to try his idea was Jean-Marie in Kalsaka village. It was the notorious drought year of 1983. He had nothing to lose. The field where he laid the stones had not produced a crop for a decade. Jean-Marie told Oxfam writer Paul Harrison: "Everybody laughed at me at first. They said it was useless. I was wasting my time. But when they saw the millet, they stopped laughing and started building lines too."

Soon collective memory kicked in. The idea was not quite as novel as everyone, including Hereford, had thought. Village elders recalled that stone walls were an old local technique for capturing rainfall. Soon the entire village was building long snaking walls across the fields, and crop yields were up 50 percent. Neighboring villages took up the idea. Oxfam began to develop a training program to bring people from across the country to learn from the villagers of Kalsaka. By the late 1980s, there were walls in more than 400 villages, catching water for farming on some 20,000 acres. Oxfam stopped counting. Its efforts were no longer needed to spread the technology. In fact, the main limitation on its spread was the supply of stones. Oxfam's last investment was a dump truck to help farmers collect them.

In the years since, researchers have occasionally returned to the scene of Oxfam's success. They are discovering that the stone walls have become the basic building block for a revival of farming across the region. In September 2002, Dutch researchers reported a widespread regreening of the Sahel. Vegetation was recovering in a wide area centered on Burkina Faso. The advancing deserts of 20 years ago were in retreat—so much so that families who had fled for coastal cities were starting to go home. A survey of farmers conducted by the Free University in Amsterdam found a 70 percent increase in yields of local grains like millet and sorghum.

Chris Reij, the Dutch scientist behind the research, said he at first assumed the cause of the revival was a simple return of the rains. That obviously played a part. But he eventually concluded that the real trigger was a change in the way farmers managed their soils and water. "The key seems to be contour bunding," he told me. "Contour bunding" is the term adopted by researchers to describe Hereford's stone walls. Thousands of acres treated with these contour stone bunds "now have trees and crops growing where nothing grew 15 years ago," he said. "Environmental rehabilitation is closely associated with villages which have undertaken these methods."

Even fields that have always been cultivated have benefited from contour bunds. UN scientists in the area estimated that bunding has typically raised yields on existing fields by 40 percent. Meanwhile, water tables are rising, wells are refilling, trees are sprouting, cattle have more fodder, and the people are healthier and fitter to work their land. There were no dams, no emptied rivers, no canals, not even pumps to bring water up from the depths. As in Machakos, a simple new method of holding water on the land, spread by word of mouth among farmers, has done what large engineering schemes and massive foreign aid budgets could not in reviving and sustaining farmland that seemed to be in terminal decline.

■ Agricultural technologists often talk as if formal irrigation were the only way to grow crops in arid and monsoon lands. It is an approach that has been encouraged by the development of "green revolution" crops that depend on regular guaranteed supplies of water. And, of course, irrigation is a managed, externally funded activity that necessarily involves teams of foreign experts—the very people who write the strategies and analyze how the world farms and feeds itself.

Today, however, there is growing interest in farming that relies more on the rain. More than half of the world's cereal production is rain-fed, after all. And formal irrigation—for reasons cultural, political, and financial— has never got going in Africa, the continent with the most hunger, the lowest farm yields, and the highest expected future population growth. Rainwater harvesting of the kind we have examined in this chapter looks set to play an increasing role in providing security for farmers stuck with unreliable rains and long dry seasons—most of the world's farmers, in fact.

More and more studies are showing what farmers knew all along. As a recent research paper from the International Water Management Institute

put it: "The yield and reliability of agricultural production can be significantly improved with water harvesting. The potential for this is very
large." It may not be far-fetched to say that the world's poor are more
likely to be kept fed over the coming decades by raising yields on rain-fed
fields than by extending formal irrigation schemes.

The Yatenga and Machakos stories are just the best-known examples,
because they have been initiated and/or analyzed by Western academics.
But studies show that such techniques are much more widespread than
previously realized out in the real, largely undocumented world of peasant farming. To take just one example, it recently emerged that up to half
of all the rice grown in Tanzania uses largely undocumented rainwater
harvesting systems, built and managed by farmers.

The advantages in such methods are that they reduce the pressure for
destructive big engineering projects to tap river water; they give farmers
greater control over their own activities; they use local materials, labor,
and expertise; they do not require extensive credit; they do not require
the sacrifice of large areas of farmland for physical infrastructure like
canals; they can be easily adapted to local conditions; and they are often
more flexible in the face of outside forces that may range from drought
to civil war.

The real question now is whether these individual examples of innova-
tive ways of handling water better in the context of more sustainable
farming methods can be scaled up to meet the world's food needs. The
answer is that it is already happening on a surprisingly large scale. Gradually, similar ideas for harvesting rainwater, using cheap and simple methods of saving water in fields, and keeping water on the land are being
revived or adopted afresh. The worldwide network of international agricultural research organizations, which took the first green revolution

around the world, is in the early stages of formulating a second green revolution based on traditional farming methods as much as on new crop
varieties.

And the Yatenga experience of stone walls is spreading all across arid
West Africa. It is no longer some development agency's project. It is the
technical cornerstone of a little-noticed revival of farming in regions once
thought to be on a one-way trip to desert, just as the Machakos region was
thought to be bound for desert half a century ago.

Not bad for a supposedly outdated technology with little to offer the
modern world.

CHAPTER SIXTEEN

Trickles and Floods

It began with a man who had time on his hands. Israeli engineer Symcha Blass had retired to the quiet of the Negev Desert in the early 1960s. One day he noticed that a large tree in the desert was growing faster than other local trees. It turned out the reason was a dripping tap that was irrigating the tree. Blass got to thinking about the virtues of dripping taps and used it to develop a system of irrigating crops using drips from narrow tubes that deposit small amounts of water right close to plant roots.

That is the story anyhow. As with most ideas, this turns out not to have been quite such a Eureka moment. A patent was filed in California back in the 1870s for a pipe with a leaking connection that was used to irrigate plants. Blass himself had used something similar to water plants in greenhouses that he ran professionally in Britain in the 1950s. But the series of modern innovations that created a simple technology that could just save the world from running out of water did begin with Blass's desert observations, which he turned into a patent application, filed in Tel Aviv in 1969.

The trick, as much as anything, was timing. Blass used modern plastics to make the supply of individual drops of water to individual plant roots an economic proposition for the first time. And he did it at a time when water shortages were for the first time becoming a serious issue in a number of desert nations with ambitions to be self-sufficient in food—not least in Israel itself. His ideas caught on. Within months, parallel patent applications and licensing agreements to use Blass's idea had been filed in southern California, Australia, and South Africa. With similar parallel developments using drip irrigation in lemon orchards and melon fields across the United States, the trickle was set to become a flood.

For virtually the whole of human civilization, we have had one response to water shortages—find more water. In recent times, that has meant building more dams, sinking more wells, digging more canals, and flooding more fields with more water. But when the rivers run dry and the wells yield nothing, we have to find another way. We have to use less water.

Irrigation of crops is the largest user of water on the planet. It takes 70 percent of our supplies, compared with the 20 percent taken by industry and the 10 percent for all domestic requirements, from drinking to toilet flushing. The figure for irrigation rises to 80 percent in developing countries and 90 percent in some of the most water-stressed nations such as Pakistan, Mexico, and Egypt. A typical field in a typical hot nation may consume 6 feet of water over a growing season. Yet the waste is phenomenal. In many places, less than half the water taken from rivers and put into canal distribution networks ever reaches fields. Less than half of what reaches fields ever gets close to a plant root. Most either evaporates into the air from canals or flooded fields, or seeps into drainage sumps or the rocks beneath the fields. To make matters worse, as the water disappears, it leaves behind a residue of salt in the soil that slowly accumulates. Eventually, unless the salt is flushed out, the soils themselves become toxic—often covered in a shiny layer of what can look disconcertingly like a sprinkling of snow in the desert.

Across the world, the great majority of irrigated crops are grown by the simple expedient of flooding the fields with water. A more wasteful system could scarcely be devised. But in the absence of any economic incentives to save water, it remains the technology of choice for hundreds of millions of farmers in countries rapidly reaching a water crunch. As Mexican rivers and wells empty, typical Mexican farmers continue to pay only 11 percent of the true cost of the water they use. In equally water-stressed Pakistan, farmers pay only 13 percent. California farmers pay as little as 2 percent. By one calculation, every acre of irrigated land in the American West receives an effective water subsidy of $400 a year.

This profligate use of water has also been encouraged by scientist and development strategists. For half a century they have developed and encouraged the use of a new generation of superyielding crop varieties, through the strategy known as the green revolution. These crop varieties are almost universally efficient at delivering more crop yield for every acre of land planted but are quite hopeless at delivering more "crop for every drop" of water used to irrigate them. As a result, in the past quarter-century, world crop yields have doubled—but world water use to irrigate those crops has tripled. "With further population rises, increased afflu-ence, climate change, and more international conflicts about water, we are going to have to think much more about how we use water," says David Pimentel, a water resources specialist at Cornell University in Ithaca, New York. Even in the United States, which is better off for water than most countries, the anticipated 30 percent increase in crop and livestock pro-duction predicted over the next 20 years "will significantly stress water resources," Pimentel says.

So it is time for a better way—to develop irrigation technologies based on minimizing use of water. Sprinkler systems, typically operated from a central pivot, are quite widely used in rich countries. But they have surprisingly high losses through evaporation. The best, and potentially cheapest, method is drip irrigation. Israel has, as in many water-saving systems, been the pioneer. Years ago, it developed a national strategy for developing both its water and agricultural resources. It was about the first country to recognize that water was the resource in shortest supply—the resource that would ultimately limits its ability to feed itself. During the past 30 years, Israel has increased its agricultural output fivefold without any increased use of water. It has done this partly by recycling urban sewage effluent to irrigate crops, but mainly through widespread adoption of drip irrigation.

Drip irrigation can take many forms. Water can be pumped down pipes under pressure and discharged into side pipes from where high-tech "drippers" deliver it to roots. Such high-tech systems can incorporate flow meters and pressure gauges to optimize distribution and keep losses to an absolute minimum. The farms of Israel, California, Tunisia, and Jordan specialize in such systems. In Jordan, a country even more water-stressed than Israel, drip irrigation reduces water use by a third and often raises yields as well. But low-tech systems are increasingly being developed for poor farmers. The simplest system is a bucket, raised a couple of feet off the ground to provide pressure and connected to a perforated hosepipe running between rows of plants. That is what Jane Ngei—whose methods in Machakos, Kenya, we reported on earlier—uses to distribute water from her hand-dug roadside reservoir. But there are many other similar ideas.

The Indians have been among the most versatile practitioners of simple drip irrigation. Some would argue that they invented it long before Blass. Many Indian farmers have recently revived a traditional half-forgotten drip irrigation system that uses bamboo pipes to distribute the water. Other Indian farmers bury simple earthenware pitchers with tiny perforations in them into the soil—a system first recorded in China 2,000 years ago and also used today in parts of Africa and the Middle East. The farmer comes around every few hours to refill the pitchers, which then simply leak their water into the root zone of the fields. Others have adopted old bicycle inner tubes, with a few extra punctures added to allow a steady drip-drip of water into the ground.

And then there is the "Pepsee." Sometime in the last decade, a farmer somewhere in central India had the idea of using the rolls of cheap polyethylene tubes being mass produced to contain the local Popsicles sold by roadside vendors. He discovered that the tubes made perfect, cheap conduits for distributing water to plants. The idea has spread, and today millions of the poorest farmers across the country use these simple tubes to irrigate their crops. They allow an acre of plants to be watered efficiently for a capital outlay of just a thousand rupees, or around $20. That is a tenth of the price of the cheapest formally engineered drip-irrigation systems, says Shilp Verma of the International Water Management Institute in Gujarat, who has researched the phenomenon. Typical water savings on each field, she says, are around 50 percent.

Can such systems save India from running out of water? Just maybe, says Raj Gupta, the Indian director of the International Maize and Wheat Improvement Center—better known as CIMMYT, its acronym in Spanish. Gupta is promoting drip irrigation as part of a suite of water-saving technologies. He reckons drip irrigation can reduce water use in the fields of northern India, the country's breadbasket, by 30 to 40 percent. He says results are best if drip irrigation is combined with other ecologically friendly and water-efficient farming techniques, such as laser methods of leveling the land. This sounds high-tech, but land leveling by means of laser techniques is rapidly coming within the price range of small Indian farmers. It can typically reduce water use by 20 percent while also raising crop yields by preventing waterlogging. Other techniques backed by Gupta include putting crops onto slightly raised beds, ploughing less, and even switching to zero-tilling, all of which again reduce water use. On his research fields, Gupta is experimenting with growing rice with less water by direct-planting into the muddy soil rather than conventional trans-planting, which requires flooded paddies.

According to the International Food Policy Research Institute (IFPRI), based in Washington, D.C., farmers have immense potential to grow "more crops for every drop." From the cornfields of Mexico to the rice paddies of China, to the lettuce plantations of California, inexpensive tech-niques—like lining irrigation canals with plastic sheeting to prevent leaks and delivering water directly to plant roots with drip irrigation—could stabilize water use in irrigation at current levels. That would be the equiv-alent of a 22 percent cut from a "business-as-usual" scenario and equiva-lent to five times the flow of the Mississippi. This strategy would involve a widespread switch to more water-efficient irrigation technologies and farming systems, the adoption of rainwater harvesting so that farmers can increase production on farms without formal irrigation systems, better controls to prevent overpumping of imperiled underground waters, and a switch to growing grains and other thirsty crops in developed, temperate countries where demands for irrigation water are less.

According to IFPRI's Mark Rosegrant, these changes could have a major effect on natural ecosystems, especially rivers and wetlands. "Many planned dams will be canceled" and a staggering 810 million acre-feet more water would be able to pass down the world's rivers. This, he says, is "the equivalent of transferring 22 percent of global water withdrawals under business as usual to environmental purposes." It would prevent the occurrence of situations like the saline desertification around the Aral Sea in dozens of countries across the world.

But will it happen? Not without dramatic changes in public policy toward water. In truth, in India, Gupta's water-saving techniques do not usually reduce the amount of water that farmers use at all. Mostly, the farmers simply take advantage of the opportunity to grow more crops, or more thirsty crops, with the same amount of water. "The trouble is that presently there are no incentives for using less water," says Gupta. "Farmers are adopting our ideas because they save fuel and cut the amount of electricity they need for pumping water from underground, not to save water."

In many places, the most water-intensive crops should simply not be grown, he believes. Much of northern India is not suitable for growing rice. Wheat and maize are much better alternatives for grain farmers. His researchers introduced me to farmers who are switching from growing rice and sugarcane to wheat, maize, and pigeon peas (*Cajanus cajan*)— saving between 70 and 90 percent of water without reducing their income. But the trend is not widespread and is unlikely to become so until farmers have real incentives to cut water use.

■ One of the major efforts needed among crop researchers today is to undo some of the damaging developments of the green revolution. In their understandable rush to produce crop varieties that could produce more food from every acre of land, the researchers behind the green revolution a generation ago ignored all other parameters in crop "yield." In particular, they ignored water. Many of the green revolution crop varieties that have kept the world fed for the past 30 years are more inefficient in their use of water than the crops they replaced. They are the single most important reason why in so many countries, the rivers and wells are emptying. We bought ourselves time with the first green revolution, but unless we follow it with a second revolution—what some call the blue revolution—to make more efficient use of water in the production of food, then the first revolution will founder. Time is short. In the fields of India, Pakistan, and northern China and Mexico, we are already seeing the first revolution start to slip away.

The successors to the first green revolutionaries have come to see that maximizing yield per unit of land is not always the top priority. "For the first time, we are starting to measure crop yields in terms of the tonnage produced for a given amount of water rather than a given amount of land," says Gupta. While land is often in short supply, so too is water. In many parts of the world, water is already a more critical constraint on the amount of food that can be produced than land. And increasing numbers of countries, in both the rich and poor worlds, will find themselves in the same boat. So the experts are back in the lab and the greenhouse developing more water-efficient ways of growing the major crops.

Rice is a clear early target. It consumes more water than any other food crop, typically twice as much as irrigated wheat, for instance. It is by far the biggest user of water across Asia, the continent with the greatest water shortages. In fact, more than a third of all the water used on the planet goes to irrigate rice paddies in Asia. But with half of all the world's rice grown in water-stressed China and India, that level of production will not be able to continue unless more water-efficient methods of growing rice are developed.

The key, say researchers at the International Rice Research Institute (IRRI) in the Philippines, is to change the traditional method of growing rice, in which farmers raise young plants in seedbeds and then transplant them to paddies that are kept flooded for the entire growing season. They want to dispense with the transplantation step and instead encourage farmers to plant seeds, presoaked in water, direct into muddy fields. Some rice varieties from China can already do this, and the researchers are trying to develop others that will grow in other countries. This innovation alone would cut water use for growing rice by around 20 percent—and requires less labor in the bargain.

Other planned innovations include replacing paddy flooding with periodic irrigation, after which the soil is allowed to become dry. These changes will need to be accompanied by extra effort to fight weeds, since one major benefit of conventional flooding is to kill weeds. But they do dramatically cut water use, especially when combined with land leveling and adding mulches to soils to cut the amount of water that leaks away through cracks. On trial plots, these techniques have resulted in savings of up to a third in water use, according to scientists at IRRI.

More controversially, scientists are working on new varieties of rice, including genetically modified varieties that do not require continuous inundation of paddies and thus cut water use by 50 percent. Researchers are targeting the new varieties for water-stressed countries across Asia, including India, Pakistan, Bangladesh, northern China, Cambodia, Laos, Afghanistan, and Indonesia.

■ All this appears immensely encouraging. There are ways, it seems, to stave off the coming world water crisis. But a note of caution is called for. We are dealing here with the operation of the water cycle. We need to be sure that by "saving" water in one area of activity, like farming, we do not create problems elsewhere in the water cycle—problems that might in the end show that our savings were not savings at all. And we need to be sure that by capturing water in new ways, such as through rainwater harvesting, we are not simply depriving others of the water.

One of the World Bank's chief advisers on water, Stephen Foster of the British Geological Survey, sees real dangers in the emerging passion for "saving" water on the farm through more efficient irrigation—particularly if the aim is not to return the saved water to nature, but to use it to grow more crops. "The idea that making irrigation more efficient will free up water for other uses has the makings of a very dangerous myth," Foster says. Much of the water being saved is never truly wasted in the first place, he argues. The water that once seeped underground from fields and canals often eventually found its way to underground water reserves—the same reserves from which millions of farmers pump water for irrigation. It was merely, in effect, being put into storage. So, as farms become more "efficient" at using water delivered to the fields, they will at the same time be putting less water into storage beneath the ground.

This, of course, is only part of the story. Not all the water percolating underground ever reaches aquifers from which it can be pumped back to the fields. And often as much water is lost from fields and irrigation canals to evaporation as is lost to seepage. Nonetheless, unless water planners take into account the fraction of water "saved" that no longer goes to recharging aquifers, then the long-term effect of "saving" water could, as Foster fears, be simply to empty the water stores even faster.

Yet in my research for this book it became abundantly clear that most farmers, agricultural planners, irrigation managers, and even environmentalists have not cottoned on to this simple fact. The repercussions could spell hydrological catastrophe in countries, like Mexico and India, that rely increasingly on underground water for their irrigation. In a recent paper, Andrew Keller of the International Water Management Institute took up the point and argued that "the classical concept of irrigation efficiency can lead to serious mismanagement of scarce water resources, because it ignores the potential re-use of irrigation return flows."

That is what seems to be happening on the banks of the Rio Grande, on the border between Texas and the Mexican state of Chihuahua. And it is happening here in a way that could have unfortunate political repercussions. After more than a decade of drought, this is a region desperately short of water. The rivers are failing because all the water is being taken by cities and farmers; and still there are acute shortages as large areas of irrigated land fall out of use because the irrigation canals are dry.

Because their farmers use practically all the water in their rivers, the Mexicans are in default of a treaty signed 60 years ago with the United States to share the rivers' flow. Come drought or flood, the Mexicans are required by the treaty to deliver at least 350,000 acre-feet of water to the border, mostly along the Rio Conchos, which drains into the Rio Grande. But for the past decade of drought, as their own reservoirs have emptied, the Mexicans have not left enough water in the rivers. They are now four years behind with their water deliveries to the border. Texas farmers are angry. But Mexican farmers shrug their shoulders. "We have no water; how can we give the Texans what we don't have ourselves?" one told me. But unless they make good soon, the U.S. administration has threatened hydrological retribution by stopping flows down another cross-border river, the Colorado, into Mexico.

So in 2003, Mexican engineers along the Rio Conchos were busy lining the canals of the largest irrigated area, at Delicias, which waters fields of alfalfa, pecan, and tomatoes for 90 miles along the river. Meanwhile, farmers were all adopting drip irrigation. Perforated hoses now run across their fields to deliver water where once farmers simply flooded the land. All this makes perfect sense. In the short term, there will be more water for the farmers in a drought-wracked landscape. The plan is to halve water use in the Delicias irrigation district, Marcial Marquez, chairman of the district, told me. "The Americans will get what we save." And the amount saved "will be nearly equal to the amount Mexico is required to send to the United States under its treaty obligations."

It sounds like a win-win situation, until you start asking questions about exactly what is meant by saved here. Do water savings to the farmers in one year amount to permanent water savings, or merely to a rearrangement of where the water is? The problem is that, as well as taking water from the Rio Conchos, farmers here also use a large amount of underground water to keep their crops growing. So what happens if the farmers put less water onto their land and line the irrigation canals? Yes, they will save some water that would otherwise evaporate. But with less water percolating underground from their fields, the underground water reserves will not be replenished by as much as before. And sooner or later they will begin to falter.

I raised this issue with Delicias irrigation operations manager Ezequiel Bueno. He dismissed the fears. So far, his farmers had seen only sporadic signs of falling water tables, he said. And the rains swiftly replenished the aquifers. But he admitted that no detailed water budget analyses had been done to assess what was happening below ground. Local researchers I spoke to were worried. "If the Mexicans believe that every drop of water that they 'save' on their farms and keep in their reservoirs can be safely sent on its way downstream to the border, then they are in for a rude shock. Some people think groundwater comes from Mars and surface water comes from Venus. They just don't realize how connected they are," says Hector Arias of the conservation group the World Wildlife Fund (WWF). The tragedy is that, to meet their immediate treaty requirements for delivering water to Texas farmers, the Mexicans are imperiling the long-term future of their own underground water reserves.

This story, without the cross-border antagonism, is in danger of being played out in different forms across the world. Wherever farmers believe that by "saving" water through more efficient irrigation they can simply use it to irrigate another field or grow a more thirsty crop, or to pay a hydrological debt, they are asking for trouble.

Don't get me wrong. There are real gains from water efficiency. It will mean less evaporation. It will improve the quality of soils by preventing a buildup of salt. It will save on pumping costs for farmers using underground water. But to believe that every drop saved on a field is somehow an addition to the overall water cycle is, as Foster put it, a very dangerous myth indeed.

CHAPTER SEVENTEEN

Making Water from Thin Air

Altering the weather to make rain is still, a half century after it was first tried in the heady early days of the Cold War, the stuff of science fiction. Maybe the American military did manage to make it rain a bit more over the rain forests of Southeast Asia to bog down their enemy on the Ho Chi Minh Trail. Maybe occasional cloud seeding over the American Midwest has, over the years, caused a cloud to disgorge its contents a little sooner here or a little later there, with benefits to some farmers and losses to others. Indian drought states occasionally announce plans to seed clouds. So do drought-hit African nations like Burkina Faso. But these seem to be more political gestures than serious efforts to produce rain.

The Israelis are more serious and have persisted with efforts to capture the moisture in winter clouds rolling in off the eastern Mediterranean. Their seeding of clouds with silver iodide is claimed to have increased rainfall by up to 15 percent. But nobody has yet demonstrated that the Israelis are making more rain, rather than simply hijacking rain that would have otherwise fallen someplace else, like Jordan. Until that happens, the technology will, to say the least, be more a source of conflict than real economic benefit. But there is a technology that can claim to be conjuring water out of thin air. Here's how.

It looked like a giant's washing line: 75 large sheets of plastic mesh suspended along a remote hilltop, known as the El Tofo Ridge, in the Atacama Desert of northern Chile. But rather than being hung out to dry, the plastic sheets were there to get wet by capturing the moisture in fogs that roll in off the Pacific Ocean. And, after a 7-year research project, they have been hailed as the first new method of providing drinking water in over a century.

The Atacama Desert is reputedly the driest place on earth. It does not rain there for years on end. But there are fogs, known locally as *camanchacas,* which drift in off the ocean. And it is here that researchers from Chile and Canada have been perfecting a technique for harvesting the moisture from those fogs. A pilot project for several years provided about 3,000 gallons of water a day for the 350 residents of Cgungungo, a small town that previously relied on water trucked in from 50 miles away. "Until we set up the water system, the town was dying," says Bob Schemenauer, who masterminded the project for Environment Canada, a government agency, and then spun off his own organization, FogQuest, to develop the idea. "But with a secure water supply, people began to return, and new houses were built."

Schemenauer's giant washing line comprised 75 double-layered polypropylene nets. Each was 40 feet by 13 feet and hung about 6 feet off the ground. They faced into the wind high above the village, where the moisture content of the ocean fogs is highest. Fog droplets are tiny: about 10 million had to accumulate on the mesh to make a single large water drop. But once formed, the drops ran down the mesh into a trough and eventually flowed downhill 4 miles to the village. The nets collected up to two-thirds of the moisture in the fogs and provided an average daily output of about 1 gallon of water per 10 square feet of mesh.

Sadly, the system is defunct today. The local authority and villagers failed to keep it up when Schemenauer departed in the late 1990s. They preferred the easy dependency of relying on the state water tanker. Nonetheless, the method is a smart and cost-effective technology that many believe could be applied in arid zones all around the world. "The only real limit is investment," says Schemenauer. "Seventy-five collectors was enough for Cgungungo, but there was room on the ridge for 750." That would have been enough to supply 25,000 gallons a day and support a population of several thousand.

Since his Chilean debacle, Schemenauer has set up similar projects in the arid mountains of Peru and Ecuador. And with funding from Canada's International Development Research Center, he has launched projects in Nepal, a mountainous country where only half the population is reached by public water-supply systems, and on the Caribbean island of Haiti, where a village on the remote Salagnac Plateau collects fog to augment water supplies in the dry winter.

An experiment in Oman, a country that relies on expensive desalination for much of its water, suggested that fog is a viable alternative for some communities there, too. The Dhofar region of Oman has fogs around 80 days a year, and nets there have produced more than 13 gallons of water from every 10 square feet on foggy days—ten times the output of the Chilean or Haitian nets. Desalination plants in the Middle East produce about half the world's desalinated water, but it costs about $7.50 to produce 1,000 gallons, with extensive capital and running expenses. Schemenauer's mesh fog-capturing system costs virtually nothing to run. In Yemen, Schemenauer is working to integrate his nets with traditional water cisterns carved into the bedrock, so they can keep the cisterns topped up when there is no rain.

Desert fogs contain large amounts of moisture. Many plants in desert regions keep moist by capturing droplets from the air. British biologists discovered a beetle in the Namibian Desert of southwest Africa that lives by catching moisture from the dense morning fogs that roll in off the Atlantic. Most intriguingly, its body has evolved a bobbled surface that turns out to be highly efficient at trapping moisture. So efficient, indeed, that the pattern has been patented and is being developed both for industrial applications and as a model in designing a better nylon mesh for catching fog.

■ Sometimes ideas just pop up out of the blue. Or, in Charlie Paton's case, out of the rain. "I was in a bus in Morocco traveling through the desert," he remembers. "It had been raining and the bus was full of hot, wet people. The windows steamed up and I went to sleep with a towel against the glass. When I woke, the towel was soaking wet. I had to wring it out. And it set me thinking. Why was it so wet?" The answer, of course, was condensation. Charlie was on the track of another unexpected, but potentially very important, method of extracting moisture from the air—and in quantities sufficient this time to irrigate industrial-scale greenhouses in the desert.

Back home in London, a physicist friend explained to Paton that the glass on the bus window, chilled by the rain outside, had cooled the hot, humid air inside the bus below its dew point, causing droplets of water to form on the inside of the window. Intrigued, Paton—a lighting engineer by profession—started rigging up his own equipment. "It occurred to me that you might be able to produce water in this way in the desert, simply by cooling the air. I wondered whether you could make enough to irrigate fields and grow crops."

Today, more than a decade on, his dream has taken shape as a giant greenhouse on a desert island off Abu Dhabi in the Persian Gulf. In it, he uses water from the ocean (which, being saline, is useless for irrigating crops itself) to cool the desert air and create liquid water. He is growing vegetables in what is basically a giant dew-making machine. In awarding Paton first prize in a design competition in 1999, Marco Goldschmied, president of the Royal Institute of British Architects, called it "a truly original idea which has the potential to impact on the lives of millions of people living in coastal water-starved areas around the world." And he doesn't even need fog.

Paton first tried out his "seawater greenhouse" in 1995 at Granadilla on the Canary island of Tenerife in the Atlantic Ocean. This arid island is crisscrossed with abandoned aqueducts that kept it green and productive until the mid-twentieth century, when the thirst of a burgeoning tourist industry emptied rivers and lowered water tables. Paton's project, funded by a European Union grant, might have revived the island's agriculture. And tourists would probably have welcomed an alternative to the increasingly saline water trickling out of the island's taps. But the EU pulled the plug on the project after what Paton insists were 3 successful years of crop production. He claims agricultural officials from southern European countries like Spain and Portugal were alarmed at the potential of his technology to undercut their own national greenhouse industries. He could be being paranoid, but I for one, having seen the lengthy correspondence, am inclined to believe him.

Paton refused to give up, however. His physicist friend Philip Davies turned the data generated in Tenerife into a model of the heat and energy flows in the greenhouse. This led to an improved design and to the greenhouse in Abu Dhabi that is now filled with cucumbers, tomatoes, arugula, and flowers, all irrigated from the desert air. The first year of trials ended in 2003, and Paton believes the technology is about to take off commercially. "My patrons in the Gulf are talking about building 400 of these greenhouses. I have a project in the Caribbean ready to go, another in Oman, and a third in South Africa," he says.

Independent observers too are optimistic. The greenhouses can produce up to a gallon of water a day for every square foot of the greenhouse, says Phil Harris, a plant scientist at Coventry University who studied the project. "Think about it. That means that, sitting in the desert, [the Abu Dhabi greenhouse] produces five times as much water as falls on Coventry. That puts it up there with some of the wettest places on Earth, such as the wetter rainforests of Papua New Guinea or central Africa or Colombia."

Harris, a leading international consultant on organic farming, says an acre of seawater greenhouses could irrigate 150,000 lettuces a year, or 20 tons of French beans, and still have 80 percent of its water left over for other uses. He says that the technology could transform the production of vegetables and horticultural crops in dozens of arid countries around the world. It would work anywhere that is hot, sunny, and running short of freshwater—as long as the place had a shoreline, of course. Paton is also fielding enquiries from ecotourist companies and others keen on building self-sufficient settlements in arid regions.

The seawater greenhouse as developed by Paton has three main parts. They both air-condition the greenhouse and provide water for irrigation. The front of the greenhouse faces into the prevailing wind so that hot, dry desert air blows in through a front wall. The wall is made of perforated cardboard kept moist by a constant trickle of seawater pumped up from the ocean. The purpose is to cool and moisten the incoming desert air. In June, for example, when the temperature outside the Abu Dhabi greenhouse is around 46°C, it is in the low 30s inside. Although the air outside is dry, the humidity in the greenhouse is 90 percent. These are ideal conditions for growing greenhouse crops. The cool, moist air allows the plants to grow faster. And, crucially, because much less water evaporates from the leaves, the plants need much less moisture to grow than if they were being irrigated in the hot, dry desert air outside the greenhouse. Paton's crops thrived on a quarter-gallon of water per 10 square feet per day, compared with the approximately 2 gallons per 10 square feet per day that would be needed if they were growing outside.

This air-conditioning of the interior of the greenhouse is completed by the second feature: the roof. It has two layers: an outer layer of clear polyethylene and an inner, coated layer that reflects infrared radiation. This combination ensures that visible light can stream through to the plants, maximizing the rate of plant growth through photosynthesis; but at the same time heat from the infrared radiation is trapped in the space between the layers, and kept away from the plants. This helps keep the air around the plants cool.

At the back of the greenhouse sits the third element. This is the main water production unit. As the humid air from the greenhouse enters the unit, it is mixed with the hot, dry air formed between the two layers of the roof. This raises the temperature of the air at the back of the greenhouse so that it can absorb the maximum amount of moisture in the next stage. Here, the air hits a second moist cardboard wall that increases its humidity as it reaches the condenser, which finally collects from the hot, humid air the moisture for irrigating the plants. The condenser is a metal surface kept cool by still more seawater. It is the equivalent of the window on

Paton's Moroccan bus. Drops of pure distilled water form on the condenser and flow into a tank for irrigating the crops.

The Abu Dhabi greenhouse more or less runs itself. Sensors switch everything on when the sun rises and alter flows of air and seawater through the day in response to changes in temperature, humidity, and sunlight. On windless days, fans ensure a constant flow of air through the greenhouse. "Once it is tuned to the local environment, you don't need anyone there for it to work," says Paton. "We can run the entire operation off one 13-amp plug, and in the future we could make it entirely independent of the grid, powered from a few solar panels." In practice, the condenser evaporates 800 gallons of seawater a day and turns it into about 200 gallons of freshwater—just enough to irrigate the plants.

Critics point out that construction costs of around $4 a square foot are quite high. They mean that the water is twice as expensive as water from a conventional desalination plant. But the comparison is misleading, says Paton. The key to the seawater greenhouse's potential is its unique combination of desalination and air-conditioning. The cool, moist air flowing through the greenhouse is very different from the hot desert air outside. It provides ideal growing conditions for the crops and for efficient use of the irrigation water. It can, says Paton, cool as efficiently as a 500-kilowatt air conditioner while using less than 3 kilowatts of electricity. Thus the plants need only an eighth of the volume of water used by those grown conventionally. And so the effective cost of the desalinated water in the greenhouse is only a quarter that of water from a standard desalinator, which is good economics.

Costs should plummet further when mass production begins, says Paton. And better sites should produce even better returns. Abu Dhabi, in fact, is far from being an ideal place to build the greenhouse. Seawater from the shallow Persian Gulf here is tepid and does a poor job of chilling the condenser plates. Colder seawater would be far more efficient both for cooling the greenhouse and for generating water. In regions such as Morocco and the arid Pacific coast of South America, cold currents bring cold water right to the surface.

Dozens of hot, dry coastal countries could benefit from the seawater greenhouse. Many struggle to feed themselves despite using all their available water for irrigation. Across North Africa and the Middle East, underground water reserves are being pumped dry. On coasts, this often means that seawater seeps into the empty aquifers, permanently polluting them. Such countries badly need new sustainable sources of freshwater.

Abu Dhabi, one of the seven oil emirates that formed the United Arab Emirates when the British left the region in 1971, may not be short of cash to buy food. But it is eager to be self-sufficient in food and to do this by growing more on desert farms. The government recently leveled 11 square miles to transform them into 3,000 irrigated farms. But watering these farms currently involves expensive and energy-intensive desalination of seawater. Paton's seawater greenhouses might replace much of this. "My hosts are planning to build another greenhouse, probably on the mainland," says Paton. "And after that, who knows? There are big plans and there is plenty of land. Provided the seawater can be piped in, you can build them even some miles away from the shore."

Best of all, the greenhouses should be environmentally friendly. "I suppose there might be aesthetic objections to large structures on coastal sites," says Harris, "but it is a clean technology and doesn't produce pollution or even large quantities of hot water."

Paton sells his technology under a license agreement with his government clients. Next stop could be the Batinah coast on the northeast shores of neighboring Oman. Once famous for its fruit trees, the Omani coastal plain has a long history of irrigated farming. But it's all gone horribly wrong, because seawater has got into the aquifer. "Even the palm trees are dying. Locally they call it Hiroshima," Paton says. He hopes a partnership with the Agricultural Experimental Station at Sultan Qaboos University to build seawater greenhouses there can turn the tide.

His latest plan is to start building among the flamingos on the flat coral-fringed island of Grand Turk in the Caribbean. The island couldn't have been better designed for a seawater greenhouse. It is perched right on the edge of a deep ocean trench, known to divers as "the wall." Within a mile of the shore the sea depth reaches around a half mile. The water temperature at that depth is around 10°C. "By exploiting the 20°C difference between the water and air temperature, you could generate very large amounts of water very cheaply," says Paton.

He also wants to position a greenhouse next to one of the planet's great ocean upwelling zones, where ocean circulation pumps cold water from the depths to the surface. One example is the west coast of Morocco. "Everybody agrees it is a great idea, but nobody wants to put in the cash," says Paton. Britain's Foreign Office is typical. It lists Paton's idea on its website as an example of "one of the things Britons are good at." But when its embassy in Morocco suggested putting up some cash to start a greenhouse there, the Whitehall mandarins vetoed it as "too risky."

The world's deserts seem poised to grow hotter and drier in the coming decades, and a greenhouse that turns seawater into freshwater—and produces more of it the hotter it gets—looks like a technology for the future. It could transform the economy of islands such as Tenerife, Grand Turk, and maybe hundreds of others in the Indian and Pacific Oceans. Certainly Paton thinks he is onto something big. "The seawater greenhouse is in the position today of wind turbines a generation ago, when they were seen as the stuff of hippies and the *Whole Earth Catalog*," he says. "But the pioneers from then are running big engineering companies today, and the technology is taking off. We have that potential." He could be right.

CHAPTER EIGHTEEN

Restoring African Hydrology

Lucy Akanboguure used to have to get up at 3:00 a.m. every day and walk to collect water from a river 3 miles away in the bush. "The earliest I got back was 10:00 a.m., which meant I was often late for work. I am a teacher," she told me. This angered the villager head teacher at her school at Kandiga village in central Ghana. But it also meant her children often went to school late, and without food for breakfast or water to wash themselves.

Lucy wanted to get on, to make a living for herself and better her family. But the daily search for water was damaging her efforts and those of her fellow women in a village where water collecting is a traditional female duty. Fetching water took up most of many women's days. And it was sometimes dangerous work, as well as arduous. "Some women were bitten by snakes during their dark dawn journeys to the river. Others fell down from fatigue—injuring themselves and breaking their water pots and calabashes," she said. In the dry season, women quarreled and beat each other in the rush for scarce water. Often they could only get dirty water, contaminated by sewage. Diarrhea, dysentery, Guinea worm, and cholera were rife.

Then a water charity showed up in the area. "I quickly organized our community and applied for assistance," Lucy remembers. "After several meetings, the project was agreed, and the first two wells were dug by hand." The community provided labor, and the water charity provided skills and materials. Today the village maintains the pumps and imposes a small charge to pay for repairs. "On the first day after the pump was installed, I woke at 6:00 a.m. and cried aloud thinking I was too late to fetch water. Then I realized my children had already woken, filled the pots with clean water and were preparing breakfast."

Of such simple stories are made the hopes of hundreds of millions of rural poor around the world. Lucy's hopes came to fruition. But more than a billion people still do not have access to clean, secure supplies of water for drinking. Typical daily consumption in the developing world is 5 gallons per head—less than half the minimum necessary for a decent life. Two billion people do not have safe sanitation, so their water supplies are at constant risk of contamination. Most are in Asia and Africa. And, despite promises at a series of world summits, the numbers are going up. The toll of this neglect of basic human needs is horrendous. The statistics dwarf even those of the AIDS pandemic. Three million people die every year from diarrheal diseases caused by poor water supplies and sanitation services, two-thirds of them children. One in two hospital beds worldwide is occupied by a person with a water-borne disease. And one in seven graves.

The World Summit on Sustainable Development held in South Africa in late 2002 promised to halve the number of people without clean water and sanitation by 2015. A modest-enough goal, you might imagine. It was reiterated in early 2003 at the World Water Summit in Kyoto, Japan. But when, in 2004, the UN Commission on Sustainable Development sat down in New York to discuss progress, it found there had been no progress. To name only the largest potential contributor, U.S. aid for water projects in sub-Saharan Africa was just $8 million a year, a tiny fraction of the tens of billions of dollars needed to do the job.

"If the world continues at this snail's pace, billions of people will remain without access to safe water or basic sanitation, with little prospect of escaping poverty," Ravi Narayanan of the UK charity Water Aid told the New York meeting. Many will continue to spend hours hauling water and will fall sick from contaminated water supplies."

But the crisis is not just about money for pipes and pumps. The other terrifying statistic echoing through the corridors of these conferences was that by 2025, two-thirds of the world's population will be living in countries where water is in seriously short supply. "All the summit agreements to improve water access will not work if natural resources of water are not conserved and water used more efficiently," says Jamie Pittock, water director of the World Wildlife Fund. "Dams and pipes alone will not solve the world water crisis. Sustainable provision starts with a commitment to protect wetlands and rivers from the damaging impacts of development itself." So, can we have our water and protect its sources too? Can we fill the world's taps without emptying its rivers?

■   During my day off from attending the 2002 World Summit, I met Margaret Futhane in a field outside Pretoria, the capital of South Africa. Back in Johannesburg, politicians from around the world were making grand promises to bring clean drinking water to more than a billion of the world's poor who currently lack this most basic requirement for a healthy life. Margaret should have been there, rubbing shoulders with the best of them, for her story could scarcely be a better advertisement for how politicians can fulfill their seemingly impossible dream—by protecting their wetlands and bolstering the planet's natural hydrology.

Margaret told me that until recently she had lived in a shack in the township of Tembisa near Pretoria. So that her family could drink and wash, she went daily to buy a few gallons of water of dubious quality from a neighbor who had a well. Like millions of poor people around the world who must buy water from neighbors or private vendors, she paid through the nose. Her pitiful pots of water cost her $18 a month. That is much more than Pretoria's middle-class households pay for an unlimited and guaranteed clean public water supply on tap 24 hours a day.

But life had recently changed for Margaret. She had moved and now lived in a proper house with clean running water in a new suburb on the edge of the city. And her water bill had fallen to less than $4 a month, for as much water as she wanted. Margaret was able to move thanks to her new job. She was running a ten-man gang rehabilitating a reed swamp near her home. That is where I met her, standing in her overalls, pitchfork in hand, supervising the men around her. The job gave her an income, of course—enough to rent her new home. But—and here is the important bit of the story—her job also indirectly helped to supply the water for her new home and those around it, for the wetland, the Rietvei, that she and her gang are helping to rehabilitate is, in effect, a natural waterworks.

It is a sponge that soaks up water in the wet season and releases it when it is needed in the dry months. Its reeds and soils clean and store water from a polluted river before it enters Pretoria's main reservoir, killing off pathogens and removing nitrates and phosphates. The swamp had previously been partly drained by farmers. Most of its reed beds had gone, and the reservoir below it had been filling with silt rather than water. "Now we are making the wetland wet again, by digging new channels to let in water and stopping up field drains," Margaret told me. Remaking the swamp was making the city's water supply cleaner, larger and more secure, so that there was enough for people like Margaret.

Here was an answer to a question left hanging by the politicians in the rarified air at their summit down the road: where would the water come from for their big dreams of providing clean water for all? The answer was not from engineering, but from nature. Margaret was improving water supplies, cleaning pollution, and alleviating poverty. She was also re-creating a water hole that is increasingly frequented by the surrounding park's population of waterbucks and rhinos.

Rand Water, the state water company, is funding rehabilitation work at Rietvei and fifty other wetlands around Pretoria. "What many may regard as useless, marshy wasteland often plays a vital role in storing and puri-fying water," said Rand Water's communications manager Leon Rossouw. "If we make use of nature's own purifying system, it will obviate the need for more expensive treatment plants." The company's engineers believe that this approach will help secure water supplies for the city, too, and ensure that many more people from the city's poor black townships can have homes with running water. And it will do it more quickly, more cheaply, and more securely than any amount of concrete pouring across the veldt.

South Africa has, most environmentalists agree, one of the most pro-gressive water policies in the world. Most countries' politicians are still fixated on large engineering solutions to their water problems. Across Africa the cry went up at the World Summit for more dams, more river diversions, more irrigation projects, and more hydroelectric plants. Yes, there is sometimes a place for dams, but dams such as that at Rietvei that work with nature rather than against it. "Summit agreements to improve water access will not work if natural sources of water are not conserved and water is not used more efficiently," Pittock told the summit.

Margaret had heard of the summit, though she knew little about what was being discussed there. But she did have a clear grasp of the nature of the water crisis. "We'll run out of water here by 2020," she told me. "We can't make more rain. So we have to manage water better."

■ Wetlands are a vital resource across Africa. When engineers claim today that 95 percent of the continent's water is unused, they are rather forgetting this. For them, water trapped behind dams is being "used," whereas that left in the rivers to flood wetlands is, in some way born only of their bizarre definitions, "wasted." It is an approach quite as mad as any adopted by Stalin or Mao in their brutal assaults on nature in the middle decades of the twentieth century. And yet it continues to find houseroom in the corridors of the World Bank and in meetings of water ministers such as the 2003 World Water Forum.

Millions of African farmers make use of small wetlands, says Arlene Inocencio of the International Water Management Institute. "While the environmental importance of wetland ecosystems is widely recognized by now, the potential role of wetlands for poverty alleviation and livelihood security for sub-Saharan Africa is still hardly explored," she told me. And properly used, there need be no conflict between traditional water use by farmers and conservation imperatives.

Recent studies have shown that the small, densely populated central African state of Rwanda, for instance, has about 400,000 acres of wetlands, more than half of which are used for agriculture. In southern Africa, small wetlands on river floodplains, known as *dambos*, are widely cultivated in countries like Malawi, Zambia, and Zimbabwe—often for small, highly productive vegetable gardens. In northern Nigeria, they are known as *fadamas*. Many farmers are adept at managing the water on their wetland plots, catching water during the monsoon season to moisten soils and grow crops during the dry months. And these small-scale systems can be adapted for use in suburban and even urban settings, where opportunist farmers move in to grow crops on abandoned boggy land, beside drainage ditches, and anywhere considered too wet for building or paving.

■ These are not just pipe dreams. During the 1990s, as we saw in Chapter 4, Nigeria systematically dammed its northern rivers, emptying green desert jewels like the Hadejia wetland. But over on the other side of Lake Chad, the authorities in northern Cameroon were taking a different approach. They were starting to undo past environmental desecration of a wetland—to the benefit of all.

The problem was the Maga Dam. It is on the River Logone, which drains out of the wet south of the country on the fringes of the giant rain forests of central Africa and makes its way across wide floodplains toward the dwindling inland sea of Lake Chad on the edge of the Sahara Desert. The floodwaters of the Logone had for millennia been the lifeblood for a thriving floodplain economy based on fishing, pasture, and recession agriculture. The Logone watered shimmering wet grasslands and replenished groundwaters. Farmers planted crops in the wet soil of its floodplain as the flood waters receded. That is, until 1979, when the Maga Dam was completed and the flood stopped dead in its tracks.

The Maga Dam stretches for 20 miles right across the floodplain of the Logone. It collects water for distribution to 12,500 acres of farms, most of them growing rice. Rice being an immensely water-hungry crop, evaporation from the dam being so great, and the water distribution network being so inefficient, not too much is grown. Only a handful of influential farmers got rich. But the loss to the downstream floodplain and the hundreds of thousands of people who depended on it has been immense. The dam stole the water from farmers and cattle pastures, cut fish yields by 90 percent, and lowered water tables across some 700 square miles of the Logone floodplain.

Pasture that had once supported 20,000 head of cattle was turned to dust. So was the Waza National Park, a home to dwindling bands of elephants, giraffes, lions, gazelles, and antelopes. Worst affected of all was the Grand Yaeres, a wetland once twice the size of Luxembourg that was probably the largest haven in the central Sahel for livestock, fisheries, and recession agriculture. And, ultimately, the dam was contributing to the emptying of Lake Chad.

Far from helping the region grow more food, the Maga Dam created a permanent hydrological drought across the floodplain. Without the regular inundations that allowed cattle to graze, crops to grow, and fish to spawn, the floodplain turned into a dust bowl. Its inhabitants left for the shantytowns on the edge of Ndjame, the capital of Chad. Or they took to poaching the last of the wildlife as the animals clustered around the region's drying water holes. It looked like the last roundup for a once-thriving ecosystem and economy. The dam's planners had ignored the role of the Yaeres wetland as a vital resource for the region's 100,000 inhabitants. They simply did not notice the huge amount of subsistence agricultural activity already going on in the floodplain. Being outside the cash economy and part of the old world that Cameroonian officials in their air-conditioned offices in the capital had personally strived to escape, it ceased to exist for them. Instead they saw it as a waste of about a million acre-feet of water a year. In their enthusiasm to green the desert, they created a desert.

The truth finally dawned, sometime in the late 1980s. International scientists and local nongovernmental organizations began to campaign for the dam's operators to revive the wetland by making regular releases of water from behind the dam during the flood season. The government eventually concurred. It turned out that sufficient releases to reflood a large part of the floodplain could be made without destroying the irrigation project. And the regular releases have resulted in a widespread revival of the region. The program has become a model for other similar plans to revive wetlands. Today, annual water releases from the Maga Dam reflood some 100 square miles of the floodplain. This is only a third of its former extent. But the releases have boosted grazing, fishing, agriculture, and wildlife. Since the first trial releases in 1994, the flooding has raised water tables. Wells are filled again. Even human health has improved, with a 70 percent reduction in water-borne diseases. Tourists are coming to the once-remote region—a region that at one time looked as if economic "progress" was destroying it.

■   We sometimes succumb to the idea that environmental thinking about rivers is somehow new. That our own ideas about renovating wetlands and floodplains, and about allowing water to remain in rivers to carry out "ecological services," are modern, born of the environmental age. Not so. The tensions between concrete-pouring engineers and those with a wider sensibility were central even a century ago, at the height of the colonial era. There were enlightened engineers even then. As a postscript to this chapter, here is the story of one of the most remarkable of them, a British colonial engineer called William Willcocks.

Willcocks was born 150 years ago in a tent beside a canal in northern India, where his father was a lock-keeper. He learned his engineering in

India before heading for Egypt in 1883. There he rose to become director-general of reservoirs and a legend on the banks of the Nile. He built the first Aswan Dam, then the largest dam in the world, and went on to revive the ancient irrigation systems of Mesopotamia and to water deserts from South Africa to India. But although knighted in 1902, he was an outsider and a man deeply troubled by the discovery that much of what he and his fellow water engineers got up to in their colonial playgrounds was worse than useless. He was perceived then as a misfit with outmoded ideas, a water engineer more concerned about silt than water, a top official who preferred the company of peasants, a team player who had turned against the team. But today, Willcocks looks more and more like an environmental visionary.

Willcocks was undeniably odd. Obituaries described him as "sallow, eyes half-closed, dressed anyway," a man for whom "dinners, dances, visits and suchlike are a wicked waste of time." For years, he "spent every day and slept every night in the fields and villages along the Nile." At Cairo's cocktail parties, they whispered that out in the villages "every fellah [*fallehin*, or farmer] knows the name Wilguks." It was not meant as a compliment.

But Willcocks's aristocratic mentor, Sir Colin Scott-Moncrieff, told many stories of his good works. One he liked to tell at dinner parties was how, when the Nile was sluggish and famine loomed in Egypt, Willcocks saw a chance to improve local food production by flooding an area of low-lying farmland. But to do it, new embankments had to be raised to divert the Nile's waters down a canal and into farmland. Some would simply have issued an ordered and retired. But Willcocks "stuck his bed on the bank of the canal, got together the peasantry of the whole province and for three days and nights worked at it till the water rose and flooded the plain." Another time he emptied a rest house to use its furniture to plug leaks in barrage gates and prevent a dangerous flood.

Willcocks's great engineering works in Egypt were the design of the Assiut Barrage, which captured Nile water for distribution across the river's wide delta region, and the first Aswan Dam. And here his troubles started. Willcocks never wanted to build the dam at all. Moncrieff had asked him to find a way to store Nile water so that more could flow down the river in the dry season and an extra crop of cotton could be grown on the Nile Delta. Like some biblical prophet, Willcocks left Cairo and spent 3 years in the desert—sleeping rough and subsisting, it was said, on rice, apricots, and whisky. Upon his return, he announced that he had found a depression in the desert, at Wadi Rayan, close to the Nile, into which he could divert part of the river's annual floodwaters, feeding it back into the river downstream in the dry season.

This was not a popular solution with the other engineers. They wanted to build a dam on the river instead. And in the end that is what Willcocks grudgingly agreed to. But he produced a dam with a difference—a first in colonial engineering. Willcocks knew that a conventional dam would prevent the river's rich silt from flowing onto Egypt's fields during the annual flood. It would wreck the fertility of the country's soils even as it irrigated them. So he devised a dam that would allow the peak of the flood, with its silt-laden waters, to pass over the dam's crest. The structure would only capture for storage the clear water that flowed later in the season.

Willcocks's Aswan Dam, 1.5 miles long and 130 feet high, was completed in 1902. It was a technical triumph, albeit a second-best as far as he was concerned. But the dam's financial backers—cotton mill owners from Manchester—soon wanted to grow yet more cotton on the delta. The dam was twice raised to supply more water. Then the cotton barons demanded a new dam, far upstream in British-ruled Sudan, to irrigate cotton fields near Khartoum.

Willcocks rebelled. He feared that the new dam would leave his own structure—and the farmers of Egypt—short of water. Sudan would be stealing the water from his "fellahs." Egypt "will be sacrificed," he wrote. To ensure that the Aswan Dam filled each year, its operators would be forced to capture the silt-laden early floodwaters, so wrecking the delta's fertility. The row got personal. Murdoch MacDonald, an imperial engineer newly arrived from Scotland, was backing the plan for the Sudanese dam. Willcocks charged MacDonald with making up key hydrological data on Nile river flows to make it look as if the dam in Sudan would pose no threat. MacDonald, he said, had grossly exaggerated the Nile's flow during dry years—and it would be during these times that the Sudan dam would threaten Egypt's water supply.

In case anyone was in any doubt, Willcocks added: "I have also charged [MacDonald] with ignorance of his profession, and concealment of public documents." The feud ended in court, where Willcocks was accused of sedition because his claims were said to have fanned the flames of Egyptian unrest. This charge failed, but he was convicted in 1921 of criminal slander and libel and left Egypt in disgrace.

The planned Sudan dam, built at Sennar, was completed in 1925. But the Egyptian "fellahs" were in luck: the succeeding decades were unusually wet. The next long drought did not come until the 1980s, by which time Willcocks's dam had been submerged by the much larger High Aswan Dam. If MacDonald did manipulate the Nile flow data, the fraud persists to this day. But whatever the merits of Willcocks's charges on this point, his insistence that the Nile's silt is as important to Egypt as its water is equally pertinent today. The new High Aswan Dam does what Willcocks feared. It prevents all silt from flowing downstream. As a result, as Willcocks predicted and as we saw in Chapter 3, Egypt's soils are denied their natural source of fertility. And Egyptian farmers are today forced to be among the biggest users of chemical fertilizers in the world.

Disgraced in Egypt, Willcocks returned to India. There he offered unsolicited advice to colonial administrators on how to use irrigation to boost declining agricultural production in famine-wracked Bengal. In a series of lectures in Calcutta, he scandalized imperial engineers all over again by arguing that their works had caused the problem.

In ancient times, the people of Bengal dug canals across the Ganges Delta. The way Willcocks saw it, the canals had a dual role. They both protected the land from inundation by capturing the floodwaters and, when the breaches were opened, allowed the silty monsoon flood to pour into the fields. The floodwaters also brought fish into the fields, where they ate mosquito larvae and so helped prevent malaria. This ingenious three-in-one technology was still in operation when the British arrived. But, in their ignorance, British engineers abandoned the canals, calling them "dead rivers," and raised the riverbanks with the aim of preventing all floods. They even prosecuted farmers who made breaches in the traditional manner to let the silt-laden water onto their fields. The results, as Willcocks pointed out, were that the soils were starved of silt, farm yields fell, and mosquitoes returned to Bengal, bringing with them a series of malaria epidemics in the 1860s and 1870s.

But Willcocks's strictures were branded the views of a crank and ignored, even though malaria continued to plague the region and famine raged in the 1940s, killing millions of Bengalis. Only in the past two decades have Indian and Bangladeshi scientists uncovered Willcocks's old lectures, which were reprinted in 1984 after being out of print for 54 years, and begun to call for a return to the old ways.

Willcocks's love of ancient engineering techniques extended to Mesopotamia—modern-day Iraq—where in 1914 he completed the rehabilitation of the Hindiya Barrage. It allowed the Euphrates to be diverted to irrigate more than 2 million acres of desert. And he went to the United States, where he gave lectures on "how the ancients would have controlled the Mississippi." They would have harnessed the river's floodplain to the cause. They emphatically would not have done what American engineers were doing—trying to stop floods by building giant levees to cut off the river from its floodplain. But Willcocks's audiences again ignored him, and his ideas were resurrected only after the massive Mississippi floods of 1993 proved him right.

While Willcocks has become an almost forgotten footnote in history, his nemesis, MacDonald, returned from Egypt to England and set up a water engineering consultancy. Its successor, now called Mott MacDonald, remains among the biggest in the world and is still at work on the Nile. One of its latest commissions is an investigation into the restoration or replacement of Willcocks's Assiut Barrage on the Nile Delta. Willcocks's last work on the river could soon be gone. But even as his physical structures slip away, his ideas are gaining a new life.

CHAPTER NINETEEN

Reviving the Wetlands

When Azzam Alwash was a boy, he went duck hunting with his father on the Mesopotamian marshes. They took an old wooden boat and rowed south from his home in Nasiriyah into one of the largest wetlands in the world—the land of the Marsh Arabs, which some believe is the geographical origin of the story of the Garden of Eden. Thirty years later, watching TV from his new home in California as U.S. troops battled for Nasiriyah, Alrash wondered at the different landscape. "I looked at the pictures of the bridges over the Euphrates. All the land behind used to be endless bulrushes and reed beds stretching for hundreds of miles. But now there is nothing green. It is totally gone."

The difference was Saddam Hussein. After the 1991 Gulf War, the Iraqi dictator drained most of the marshes, an area twice the size of the Florida Everglades. And then he stopped the Tigris and Euphrates, the two great rivers that filled the marshes, from replenishing the marsh waters. Within the space of a few months, Saddam's engineers diverted almost the entire flow of the Euphrates into a large drainage canal, known as the Third River, which they then connected to the sea. On the Tigris, they built locks and sluices and raised banks to halt the river's outflow into the marshes. It was an epic work of destructive civil engineering that turned the ecological jewel of the Middle East into a salt desert. And, as Saddam intended, it drove out most of the 50,000 Marsh Arabs, many of whom had joined the abortive uprising against him in 1992. The outside world only learned about these efforts in 1993, when satellite images revealed a sudden diminution of the wetlands.

At their fullest extent the freshwater lakes, reed beds, and endless waterways of the Mesopotamian marshes once covered almost 8,000 square miles, stretching north and west from the southern town of Basra toward Nasiriyah and Baghdad. Half a million people relied on the marshes to grow rice, catch fish, hunt otter and birds, gather reeds, and graze water buffalo. Besides the Marsh Arabs, who were made famous in Wilfred Thesiger's 1964 travel book of the same name, they included people such as Alwash and his father, who lived around the fringes of the marshes.

Western governments cried foul about the destruction of the marshes. Human rights activists described the actions as attempted genocide against the Marsh Arabs. But, embarrassingly for some of his critics, Saddam's plan to drain the marshes was not new. It was first put forward by British engineers working for the Iraqi government almost half a century before. A report written in 1951, which I unearthed on a dusty shelf at the Institution of Civil Engineers in London, advocated a number of the building projects that were subsequently pursued by Saddam. In particular, it described an array of sluices, embankments, and canals on the lower reaches of the Tigris and Euphrates that would be needed to "reclaim" the marshes.

The document was called *Control of the Rivers of Iraq*, and it had been published in 1951 by the Iraqi Irrigation Development Commission. It was written by a senior engineer formerly with the British Indian administration, Frank Haigh. In a chapter on "the reclamation of the marshes,"

Haigh outlined a plan to divert the Euphrates into a "Third River" and to place sluices across the outlets of the main "distributor" rivers that carried most of the Tigris's flow into the marshes. He argued, as did most water engineers of his day, that water allowed to dissipate in the marshes was wasted. That natural marshland was a waste of land that could be used for more productive activities, like irrigated agriculture. Haigh wanted to capture the marsh water for irrigation. "For the reclamation of the marshes it will ultimately be necessary to escape the whole of the [rivers' flow] directly to the sea," he wrote.

Following the publication of Haigh's report, construction of parts of the Third River, which ran from Baghdad to Basra, was begun under British supervision in 1953. More works were completed in the 1960s under the supervision of the British consultancy Murdoch MacDonald, now Mott MacDonald. "We did the early design work for the Third River," Bill Pemberton at Mott MacDonald told me in 1993. "We built our bit, about 15 miles. The rest they now seem to have done themselves."

Saddam's works during 1993 certainly bore a striking resemblance to the Haigh plan. His engineers raised embankments and created a canal, often more than a mile wide, that sealed the river off from the surrounding marsh. The canal disgorged into the empty bed of the Euphrates near its confluence with the Tigris. Its effect was to capture almost all the flow that once filled the Amara Marsh, one of three that make up the domain of the Marsh Arabs. He also dried out the Hammar Marsh, which lies to the east of the Tigris and extends over the border with Iran, by diverting the Euphrates into the completed Third River.

According to Saddam's chief engineer, Zuheir Abbas, the Third River was intended to "reclaim" more than half a million square miles of salt-encrusted fields—enough to increase Iraq's crop production by up to 50 percent. Saddam himself proclaimed that it would be "a welfare artery that will renew the life of our people." That certainly was its purpose under the Haigh plan. But in the hands of Saddam, it was used to divert the waters of the Euphrates away from the marshes. Saddam never grew a thing in his drained marshes. He emptied them of people as well as water—a job completed by torching villages and pouring poisons into the marshes. By 2003, as Saddam took his final stand against the Americans, some 93 percent of the marshes were dry, salt-encrusted wasteland, and scientists feared that the rest could soon be gone.

Alwash—who is, like his father before him, a civil engineer—would probably have had to work on Saddam's drainage project if he had not left Iraq for the United States in the late 1970s. But as war ended in Iraq in the spring of 2003, Alwash called for an international effort to bring back the landscape of his childhood as soon as stability returned to the country. He and his American wife, Suzie, a geology professor, became the moving forces behind an ambitious plan to re-create the ancient marshes. Their Eden Again project gained support from the U.S. State Department and aid officials, from the United Nations Environment Programme (UNEP), and from the Marsh Arabs themselves. The couple recruited hydrologists, ecologists, and engineers to draw up plans for what would be the most extensive wetland rehabilitation ever attempted anywhere on Earth.

But while Alwash and his wife lobbied the new government in Baghdad and assembled an international coalition to aid the effort, the Marsh Arabs began to go it alone. In late 2003, the first Marsh Arabs began to return to the marshes and started to reflood patches of marsh wherever and whenever they could. They shut down pumping stations and attacked dykes with farm implements and municipal earth-moving equipment. In the first stages, the reflooding was small-scale: just 75 square miles, a hundredth of the former marshland area of 7,600 square miles. As Alwash put it on a visit in late 2003: "On the ground these areas seem enormous— water as far as the eye can see—but when located on satellite images we see how small their extent actually is."

It was not clear how much further the Marsh Arabs could proceed without access to much more equipment and engineering expertise. But while many applauded their efforts, others warned that there were real dangers in such a piecemeal approach. "The one thing we cannot do is just plug up Saddam's canals and let the water flow back into the marshes," Alwash had told me before the Marsh Arabs started work. The desiccated soil is too fragile for that, he said. It is caked in salt left behind as the last of the water evaporated. If saline water were allowed to fill the marshes' depressions in the first flush, the marsh could be poisoned forever. "It will have to be a phased approach, starting with small demonstration areas near the main rivers and working into the center of the marshes," agreed Tom Crisman, director of the University of Florida's Center for Wetlands.

Weeks later, there were early signs that Alwash was right to fear that hasty reflooding could create a salt desert in place of a sandy one. By autumn 2003, the Hammar Marsh, on the southern fringes of the former wetlands where the Euphrates and Tigris Rivers join, appeared to be turning into a salt pan because there was no outlet for the new water being released into the marsh. The water simply sat in the desert evaporating in the sun. Reed beds, which had briefly flourished when the waters returned, began to die again as salt levels rose through the long summer. Meanwhile, the Amarah Marsh in the far north on the Tigris had become far saltier than the Tigris River, and in places almost as salty as seawater.

Such damage, like the flooding itself, remained in mid-2004 small in scale. But the big question now is how much of the ancient marshes can be re-created? And if re-creation can be done, how many of the Marsh Arabs will want to go back permanently? Iraq's new Ministry of Water Resources declared marshland restoration its number one priority and set up a center for the restoration of the marshes. It brought in the Eden Again project and international agencies like the United Nations Environment Programme to offer advice. Crisman says: "It's probably the most ambitious wetland rehabilitation ever attempted. And we will be trying to put back a culture as well as an ecosystem. I don't know of a precedent for that. But it can be done, I am sure." He believes it could become a precedent for reviving many other natural water reservoirs as the world staves off growing water shortages.

But it is not just a matter of re-creating the hydrology of the marshes themselves, for the marshes had not, it transpired, been undone by Saddam's drains alone. The construction of Turkish dams on the headwaters of the Euphrates and Tigris over the previous two decades had aided Saddam. A series of giant dams, including the vast Ataturk Dam on the River Euphrates, had cut the total amount of water coming down the rivers by some 20 percent. And it had greatly diminished the spring flood peak that was essential to the annual flooding of the marshes. Hydrologists warned that with more construction planned on the Tigris, dams could eventually cut the flow of the rivers into Iraq by up to a half and eliminate the spring flood.

And Iran was implicated, too. Much of the last remaining wet area, the Hawizeh Marsh, close to the Iranian border, had dried up only in 2001 and 2002, after the impoundment of an Iranian dam had stopped the flow of the River Karkheh, the main source of water for the Hawizeh. The Hawizeh is the last refuge for species of plants, fish, and animals that could recolonize the marshes. Ecologists warn that if those species—which include animals found nowhere else, such as the smooth-coated otter—are lost, the natural ecosystem of the marshes will no longer be able to regenerate. With more dams being built all the time, says UNEP scientist Hassan Partow, "the whole region is in a water crisis."

Re-creating the marshes will require the reestablishment of proper river flows all down the Tigris and Euphrates, mimicking the spring flood pulse as well as maintaining overall flows. And that requires the cooperation of Iraq's upstream neighbors. Scientists at UNEP believe that a successful rehabilitation will require both a new treaty to share the waters of the rivers between the nations of the region and an Iraqi government that is willing to allocate some of its share for the marshes.

UNEP spent much of 2003 quietly pressing the countries sharing the rivers—Iraq, Turkey, Syria, and Iran—to draw up a water-sharing treaty. In September 2003, Iraq's water minister, Abdul Latif Rasheed, called for talks with Turkey and Syria to "reach an agreement that divides water among the three of us in a just manner." Under such an agreement, upstream countries would be required to release water from their dams in spring to mimic the natural flood flows that once filled the marshes. But there were few early signs that Turkey and Syria would be amenable to such requests. During a conference at the height of the U.S. invasion of Iraq in early 2003, Turkey outright rejected calls for an international treaty to cover the Tigris and Euphrates.

Politics, as much as hydrology, will ultimately decide the fate of the marshes. But while that plays out, Alwash has a dream. "My wife and I go kayaking on the weekends here in California," he told me from his American home as the U.S. forces settled into Baghdad. "I keep telling her: one day you'll see what a real wetland is. My dream is to go kayaking on the Iraqi marshes with her and my kids—just as I went with my father."

■ Wetland rehabilitation is starting to become a growth industry world-wide. The folly of destroying such fecund water systems and the tangibility of the benefits to be gained from reviving them are such that even the most water-stressed countries can see the pluses. Thus Jordan a decade ago began work to revive its Azraq Oasis. The oasis formed the wet heart of a wide desert basin where the region's sparse rains gathered. The oasis is the wettest spot in that part of the Middle East and probably one of the longest continually populated places in the entire region. Its archaeological remains go back 200,000 years. In a good year, the seven wadis that meet there, and the underground water channels that followed them, brought around 20,000 acre-feet of water a year into the oasis. Farmers extracted a similar amount each year to irrigate their fruit trees, vegetables, and grain crops. The oasis got by, and its lakes, marshes, abundant bird life, and eighth-century castle were a growing tourist attraction on the road from Amman to Baghdad, in the days when plenty of people made the journey.

But that was before, in the late 1970s, the fast-growing Jordanian capital of Amman, which had lost much of the flow of the River Jordan to Israel, first built a water pipeline to the Azraq Oasis. Within a few years Amman too was taking 20,000 acre-feet a year out of the oasis. With abstraction now twice the recharge rate, the oasis began to die. Its springs dried up, and the only water reaching the surface was salty water from a deep aquifer. By 1993, slow-burning fires began to work their way through the marshes, leaving a pall of smoke over the dead and dying vegetation. Farmers gave up; tourists no longer came. And the saline water left in the aquifer was swiftly becoming useless to both farmers and the people of Amman.

The following year, under international pressure, Jordan began to draw up recovery plans. Once the decision was taken, it emerged that much of the destruction had been unnecessary. Just 8 miles away was another small basin area that still contained a surplus of water. Engineers began piping it, at a rate of up to 1,600 acre-feet a year, to replenish the oasis lakes. The surrounding wadis were cleaned and deepened to maximize flow of water into the oasis during the rainy season. Soon the water table was rising. Now there are water buffalo and blue-necked ostriches and Nubian ibexes and dragonflies in the oasis again, and the indigenous killifish has been successfully reintroduced. The replacement aquifer will not last forever, of course, and Amman still needs a permanent, sustainable source of water. But the unique Azraq Oasis has at least been saved for now.

Conclusion

CHAPTER TWENTY

Battle for the New Agenda

The man from Manila had a bottle of brown liquid. He was inviting the representatives from the transnational water corporations to take a sip. "It comes from one of your water pipes," he said. Neither Gerard Payen nor Antoine Frerot, the chief executive officers, respectively, from Suez and Vivendi, the two French water companies that supply the capital of the Philippines, was drinking. "You won't drink your own water," the man from Manila mocked. The CEOs and their angry customers were in Kyoto for the world's largest-ever conference on the world's water. And the CEOs were attending a panel to demonstrate, in a series of mind-numbingly bland statements, that they were inclusive, caring, and committed to dialoguing with their customers and critics. But not, it seemed, to drinking with them.

As the United States and Britain went to war over Iraq in March 2003, there was another war going on in Japan—over the future of the world's water. And the corporate armies behind the privatization of water supplies won a key battle. They captured control of the world's agenda for meeting UN development goals in water and sanitation that had been agreed upon at the Johannesburg World Summit on Sustainable Development the previous year. Ministers from more than a hundred countries were at the World Water Forum in Kyoto. Its intended purpose was to put flesh on the bones of the World Summit's pledge to cut from 2 billion to 1 billion the number of people worldwide without clean drinking water or modern sanitation. With a doubling of investment in water infrastructure promised in the coming decade, control of the purse strings matters.

The promised plan never materialized. But in their minimalist twenty-seven-paragraph statement, the ministers gave their assent to the ever-greater involvement of private money and private funds in managing the one resource without which none of us can live. The privatization push, hatched by industrialists and their friends at the World Bank, flew in the face of the growing anger at the power and performance of the water barons, and in particular the handful of companies—headed by Suez, Vivendi, and Britain's Thames Water—that have been assembling port-folios of water supply contracts across the globe. But the politicians said it was the only way to unlock the funds to meet their goals.

The big-three international water companies have created chaos in their first forays into developing countries. They scented easy profits in running municipal utilities by slashing workforces and raising prices. But they came unstuck—and left their hosts to bail them out and pick up the pieces. Take Suez. Through its local company, Mayniland, in Manila, Suez tried to impose massive price increases on its water customers after taking over there in the mid-1990s. When there were protests at soaring charges and filthy water, the company stopped paying its fees for the concession. And then in December 2002, it announced that it was walking away, abandoning the concession and claiming $300 million in compensation for its "investment." In Argentina, Suez wrote off $500 million on a contract to supply Buenos Aires with water when the peso collapsed and asked the government to cough up the difference. In January 2003, there were riots in Jakarta, the capital of Indonesia, over planned price hikes by Suez and its partner in the city, Thames Water. In Bolivia and Ecuador, South Africa and Panama, "water riots" have become a new feature of the political scene following privatization.

When water charges doubled in the Argentinean province of Tucuman after Vivendi took over supplies for a million people, protests became so fierce that the company pulled out. "They were not making any investments, just raising the price of water," said one recipient of its bills, Jorge Abdala in San Isidro de Lules. In the French towns of Saint-Denis and Réunion, and in Milan, Italy, Vivendi has received convictions for bribing local officials to obtain water contracts. And in Turkey, government officials are under investigation into how they came to draw up a contract with Thames Water in which the state foots the bill for water supplied to the city of Izmit that customers won't buy because Thames is charging prices they cannot afford.

■ According to the industry newsletter *World Water Report* in early 2003: "Across the board, private sector water activity overseas is in retreat. It is impossible for investors to secure a quick return." Nobody doubts that this retreat is temporary and that the industry will try again, having secured changes to the financial rules for its investments. Officials at Britain's Department of Trade and Industry told industry leaders in February 2003 that global business worth $600 to $800 billion is up for grabs in the coming decade, thanks to the UN's millennium targets.

But people who know about water and sanitation rather than money trash claims that private cash and private business can, or even might want to, crack the millennium targets. Sir Richard Jolly, a leading public health economist, creator of the UN Development Reports, and chairman of the Geneva-based Water Supply and Sanitation Collaborative Council, says that commercially viable projects "can only deliver sanitation to a tenth of the billion-plus people targeted by the UN." Most of the rest "are simply too poor to be attractive to private enterprise." Ministers, said Jolly, should be rejecting privatization and backing "low-cost and small-scale schemes in rural and poor urban areas." Such schemes would reach more people and cost only a tenth as much as conventional big-engineering approaches.

Water industry guru Peter Gleick takes the same view. In late 2003, he castigated the World Water Forum's claim to need $180 billion a year all the way to 2025 to meet the UN goals. "This figure is based on the assumption that future global demand for water and water-related services will reach the level of industrialized nations and that centralized and expensive water supply and treatment infrastructure will have to provide it. If we focus on meeting basic human needs for water for all with appropriate-scale technology, the cost instead could be in the range of $10 billion to $25 billion a year for the next two decades—a far more achievable level of investment."

Gleick advocates what he calls the "soft path" in water management, which avoids enormous infrastructure investments. The more affordable and practicable solutions Gleick favors are likely to involve mainly simple local technologies like rainwater harvesting and drip irrigation. Throughout the developing world these methods involve the kinds of locally appropriate, small-scale technologies and culture-based practices described in this book. They do not primarily involve the supply of huge volumes of water down pipes and canals from large dams—the kind of things that international water companies may be good at arranging. They require more efficient use of water already available locally, through management of the landscape to conserve water and through efficient use of water in fields. "Simple rainwater harvesting systems can double the water available to poor villages in arid India through the long dry season. Two crops can grow where only one grew before. And smart low-tech systems of delivering that water to the roots of crops can mean that twice as many fields can be planted. Such systems can transform the lives of billions of people across the planet," Gleick argues.

■   In the industrialized world, there are also enormous opportunities, with global repercussions, to manage water better. We can all make choices, for instance about how we outfit our homes. Almost every house could be fitted with gutters and a tank to capture rainwater from the roof and maybe the yard as well. You probably won't want to drink it, but you can use it to irrigate garden crops or clean the car and even, with a little plumbing, to flush toilets. And we can use water more efficiently. The United States in particular has made big progress in cutting domestic water use by adopting low-flush toilets. The amount of water used to flush the nation's toilets has been cut by three-quarters in the past two decades. Similar savings can be made in a similar manner by redesigning everything from shower units and public urinals to industrial processes.

There is a rather large "but" here, however. Almost anything we do to save water at home is a drop in the bucket compared with the role our shopping and eating habits play in our personal water use. By my calculations, a typical meat-eating Westerner consumes, indirectly through Western consumption patterns, around a hundred times his or her own weight in water every day. You could, for instance, fill several bathtubs or take several dozen showers with the water it takes to grow the cotton to make a single T-shirt. Don't ask about the amount of water it takes to manufacture a car or computer—or to cool the turbines at your neighborhood power plant. But the biggest day-to-day component for most of us is food, especially grains and vegetables grown using irrigation and meat raised in feedlots or on irrigated pasture.

David Pimentel is a water resources specialist at Cornell University in Ithaca, New York. He has calculated the quantities of water needed to bring a range of foods to the dining table in the United States. His statistics are staggering. They reveal that more than 200 gallons of water are needed to grow a typical pound of rice, the most thirsty grain crop, whereas around 130 gallons are usually needed to produce a loaf of bread and 60 gallons to yield a pound of potatoes. The disparity in the amounts of water used to produce different meats is even greater. A pound of broiler chicken needs more than 400 gallons of water, whereas a pound of beef from cattle fed on irrigated fodder or grazed on irrigated pastures needs a staggering 8,000 or more gallons. That means that a plate of beef and rice needs around twenty times more water than a plate of chicken and potatoes. Food for thought.

More water needs to be recycled. Almost every drop of water that goes into urban areas leaves again in a contaminated form, usually in sewage effluent. For most urban areas this is a major problem, often dumped into rivers that become festering and disease-ridden sumps. But out in the countryside, recycled water can be a boon. There are few official statistics on how much of the world's farmed land is watered using municipal sewage effluent, but the figure is probably well in excess of 2 million acres and growing. Nor are there statistics on how productive the land is, but sewage is a good source of free nutrients; and most wastewater farming is close to urban areas where markets for produce like vegetables are abundant and where local productivity is normally high.

Two countries with heavy use of wastewater for irrigation are Mexico, which alone may account for 1.5 million acres, and Israel, which has a statewide program of treating urban wastewater so that 70 percent of it is reused to irrigate crops on farms. Indeed, wastewater now amounts to almost a fifth of all that country's available water supplies. Another proud practitioner is Singapore, which in 2003 announced plans to lace its reservoir water—much of which is bought from neighboring Malaysia—with 2.5 percent recycled sewage effluent.

We consumers will find it hard to know how much water is used in growing our food. There is a lot of stuff written on most food packaging about the nutritional contents, but nothing to tell us how much water it took to grow and process the food. In any case, the real action on many water issues can take place only at a state level. Governments have to take water saving and recycling as seriously as they have previously taken water supply.

■   One big issue here is water pricing. States around the world urgently need to change the way that water is charged for. In much of the world, water is still seen as essentially a free resource. Charges, even for the pipes that bring the water or the treatment works that clean it, are resented. Farmers in particular are able to exert huge political influence to keep down the prices charged for the enormous amounts of water than they use. This cannot go on. How motivated we are to save water inevitably depends on how expensive our water is.

Countries as different as Morocco and China have recently made significant cuts in water demand by raising prices. But most countries still resist realistic pricing, even though the evidence is that it works. In general, a 10 percent rise in the price of water will reduce water use by 1 to 2 percent among irrigating farmers and by 5 percent or more among both domestic and industrial urban users.

There are important issues of equity and national survival here. If India, for instance, suddenly decided to make farmers pay the economic price for their irrigation water and for the electricity used in pumping water, much of the country's rural population would instantly go out of business. Tens if not hundreds of millions of refugees would starve or head for the cities. It would amount to a national meltdown. But modest price increases that encourage more efficient use of water are essential.

And, at least in urban areas, the issue of equity is not as straightforward as it might seem. Charging more for water would in many cases reduce the amount that tens of millions of the poorest city-dwellers spend on water. How come? Because run-down urban water supply networks charging low prices are typically the networks that have the least penetration into poor suburbs. In practice, these networks only reach middle-class suburbs, so the middle classes end up getting all the subsidies. Meanwhile, with low prices, there is no money to invest in supplying the poor neighborhoods. The poor have no chance of benefiting from public water supplies, subsidized or not. Their only choice is to buy from private vendors hawking from shanty streets and alleyways or selling from standpipes on the roadside.

The subsidies to the middle classes in many megacities in the developing world are huge. Take the Indian capital, Delhi. It costs the city utility around 30 rupees to capture, treat, and distribute 1,000 gallons of water; yet the recipients pay less than 3 rupees. That is a big subsidy. Yet in Delhi, which is fairly typical of Asian cities and rather better than African ones, only about half of urban residents have connections to their city water utilities. The rest of the population, mostly the poorest, who could most use the subsidies, instead have to get water from informal, usually private sources. And they pay through the nose.

The Tanzanian capital of Dar es Salaam provides another good example. The city's population has soared to 3 million in recent years, but the water supply network has not been extended or renovated for 30 years. The city water utility has only 100,000 paying customers. And, with leaks and other unmetered losses such as illegal connections running out of control, only a third of its paying customers receive water for seven days a week. Meanwhile, most of the thousands of illegal connections to the water mains are made by water vendors, who use them to extract water to sell on the streets. This is the water that perhaps three-quarters of the city has to buy in order to live. For them, a 4-gallon can of water typically costs 10 cents—more than ten times the rates charged by the city utility. This is madness. But it is not unusual. One study of water prices in seventeen cities in developing countries found that water vendors charged anything from five times more in Abidjan, in the Ivory Coast, to eighty times more in Karachi, Pakistan.

■   The problem with privatization of water, it should be said, is not primarily private-sector involvement; it is the hijacking of water supplies by Western engineers and inappropriate Western technical solutions. The new "soft path" in water management requires an entirely different set of skills from those on offer from the international water companies.

In the late 1990s, the World Bank had attempted to meet many of the concerns about the destructive effects of dams with a virtual embargo on new funding and by establishing a World Commission on Dams that was highly critical of past practice. Many had thought that this sea change would herald the onset of a new global push toward "soft" solutions. But the ministers in Kyoto ignored all this. They had been hoodwinked by the cheerleaders for the creeping privatization of world water policy.

Right now, 95 percent of the world's water is still supplied by public bodies. And most sewage disappears down public sewers. But private companies want to operate many plum urban supply systems and build others. They hear the words of people like Asit Biswas, a leading industry consultant for 20 years, who told the Kyoto meeting that "the world is heading for a water crisis that is unprecedented in human history; water development and management will change more in the next 20 years than in the last 2,000 years." And they see the UN millennium pledges—and the tacit endorsement by ministers in Kyoto of the push for privatization—as the lever to open up the world of urban water supply to private capital and corporate profit.

Pushing the case for the privatization agenda is the World Water Council, which helped organize the Kyoto water summit. It calls itself an "international water policy think tank dedicated to strengthening the world water movement for an improved management of the world's water resources and water services." It was set up in 1996 and is based in Marseilles—naturally enough since it derives much of its money from French water companies. Most of the council's 300 members are rich-world bankers and industrialists, among them the promoters of two of the world's most controversial water megaprojects, the Sardar Sarovar Dam on the Narmada River in India and the network of dams being built by Turkey in Kurdish southeastern Anatolia. But the council claims to speak for the world on water and to have created a "consensus for action" on meeting UN water and sanitation targets.

Many reject this consensus. "The World Water Forum is an attempt to control international debate on water," said Joan Carling of the Cordillera

People's Alliance in the Philippines. "The Council has hijacked the water agenda of the world, but knows nothing about how the hydrological cycle works. They are interested only in the commodification of water," said Indian environmentalist Vandana Shiva. These critics say that the World Water Council has two current priorities, both endorsed by the forum and the ministerial declarations at its conclusion. One is to privatize. The other is to revive the building of large dams and to trash the findings of the World Commission on Dams about their substantial, and growing, downside.

"There has been a coordinated effort against the World Commission's report," says Paddy McCully of the International Rivers Network. That effort had as its first target the World Bank, the world's largest funder of large dam projects over the past half century and chief instigator of the World Commission's deliberations. And that effort swiftly bore fruit. In February 2003, just two years after the commission published its coruscating findings, the World Bank announced a new water strategy that put dams back on its shopping list for the first time in almost a decade.

Meanwhile, in the wider world, the dam builders began a charm offensive. Dams, they told anyone who would listen, are essential to deliver the water, sanitation systems, and electricity needed by the poor. "The world will need to double its large dams," declared Mahmoud Abu Zeid, Egypt water minister and president of the World Water Council, during his opening address to the World Water Forum. "800,000 DAMS ARE NOT ENOUGH" was the headline on one official Forum press release. Dams equal development, the industry argued. Ethiopia had one-hundredth of the water storage capacity per head of the United States or Australia—13,000 gallons a head in Ethiopia, compared with 800,000 to 1.3 million gallons in the United States or Australia. Dams, it was implied, would prevent drought.

Yes, mistakes had been made in the past, the industry agreed. But that was in the past. In the twenty-first century, they would build better and consult with affected communities. "Look, countries need infrastructure, and that includes dams," Kristalina Georgieva, environment director at the World Bank told me a few months later. "And that need will grow with global warming. Not to admit that is dishonest. The bank could opt to protect its rear end and stay away from these issues. But we are here to solve countries' problems."

All the talk from the new generation of dam builders about consulting with local communities before building dams in the future seemed to amount to very little with William Cosgrove, the World Water Council's vice president, when I interviewed him in Kyoto. "What does this participatory exercise mean? Is it pro forma? What if the dam is in the country's interest, even if the locals don't want it?" he asked rhetorically. "We can't go on not building dams because some of the old ones turned out badly."

■   While the rhetoric for large dams tends to revolve around providing clean drinking water for the world's poorest, the reality of the engineers' plans is usually more about water supply for large cities and hydroelectric engineering projects. And this is true no more so than in Africa, where the industry's model of centralized water supply through Western-style structures is hopelessly inappropriate, ludicrously expensive, and immensely destructive of existing methods of using natural water supplies. It is clear, too, that those who advised ministers at the World Water Forum had little notion of how water is currently used in Africa. They told ministers in one widely disseminated report that in Africa, "available water resources are grossly underused. Only 3 percent of its renewable water is withdrawn annually . . . in a continent where 40 percent of the population has inadequate access to water." The message was clear to all: withdrawal equals use.

What nonsense. The data it quotes exclude the huge economic and social benefits African farmers gain from irrigating their crops and feeding and watering their animals on floodplains and in wetlands without "withdrawing" water at all. And it ignores the millions more Africans who capture and use rainwater without it going near a river or large dam. But because these people are not "withdrawing" water in the sense that a Western water engineer understands it and are not making a commercial profit out of water technologies in a way that a Western economist can compute, their lives and water management systems simply cease to exist when water is discussed at the high ministerial tables.

Worse still, most dam builders are not primarily interested in supplying water at all. All across Africa, where the real need is to meet basic human needs among poor rural communities, there are grand schemes afoot to spend scarce development money not on water supply at all, but on hydroelectricity. The engineers want to use the power of some of the world's greatest rivers to light its cities.

Most schemes are being promoted under the banner of the New Partnership for Africa's Development (NEPAD), which is being described as a "Marshall Plan" to bring development to Africa. Set up in 2002 by African leaders, it is backed by the G-8 club of rich nations; Tony Blair called its fulfillment "my passion." South African president Thabo Mbeki promises that NEPAD will deliver "a practical program that changes the lives of the masses of Africa away from despair" and that it would meet the targets set at the World Summit. But what will it mean in practice? The projects discussed behind the scenes at NEPAD meetings at the UN in New York look very different from those envisaged in Johannesburg.

The biggest scheme, strongly backed by Mbeki, is the creation of an Africa-wide electricity grid. At its hub would be the world's largest hydroelectric scheme, at Inga Falls on the River Congo. Here the river drops 330 feet, promising huge amounts of energy for powering turbines. The $6 billion Grand Inga Project envisages fifty-two separate electricity-generating units, each the size of a large conventional power station. They would have a combined generating capacity ten times that of Africa's largest existing dam at Aswan in Egypt and more than twice that of China's controversial Three Gorges scheme. The scheme is the brainchild of South African energy conglomerate Eskom and could, it is claimed, meet the current electricity demands of the entire continent.

Connecting Inga Falls even to Africa's main population centers would cost more than $10 billion. The first power lines would link it to South Africa via Angola and Namibia, a distance of 2,000 miles. Next it could go 2,500 miles north through the Central African Republic and Sudan to Egypt. Nigeria wants to take Inga power to West Africa. And Eskom also talks of exporting power to Europe, via Spain. Technical advances in high-voltage electricity transmission, along with the initiatives to end the long-running civil war in the Democratic Republic of the Congo, have made the project possible. Construction could begin as early as 2005, say its backers.

All this may turn out to be pie in the sky, but such dreams of mega-engineering are diverting the attention of people who should be thinking about meeting the needs of Africa's poor. What is certain is that the scheme—and other similar projects like Ugandan president Yoweri Museveni's plan to build a giant hydrodam at Bujagali Falls, a popular tourist attraction on the Nile—would gobble up large amounts of NEPAD's anticipated budget of $60 billion. And it could scarcely be further from the goal of small-scale sustainable energy projects discussed at the World Summit, where the talk was of bringing electricity to rural people through local wind and solar power projects.

Power grids, most agree, will never reach the hundreds of millions of Africa's rural poor, whose needs NEPAD is supposed to be addressing. "These guys just don't get it," says McCully, who has become a hate figure for the dam builders. "They don't understand, or refuse to acknowledge, that there is another development agenda that does not revolve around large-scale infrastructure, that puts at its heart people with democratic rights rather than just statistics."

■ In the middle of April 2004, something odd happened. Chinese premier Wen Jiabao called a temporary halt to work on a giant new hydroelectric dam that would drown an area described as China's Grand Canyon. The canyon is on the River Nu, which, after it passes south into Burma and Thailand, is known to the rest of the world as the Salween. The premier's postponement of engineering works while new studies of potential adverse impacts was a potential reprieve for one of China's last wild rivers. Was it a more significant change of heart from the country that houses half the world's large dams? Could be. Such projects "cause great concern in society," said the premier, the successor to the notorious dam enthusiast Li Peng, who pushed forward both the Three Gorges Dam and the south-north river transfer scheme.

The premier's statement did seem to be part of a pattern. It came only weeks after China's State Council Energy Research Center called for a new emphasis on reducing demand for electricity rather than on building ever more hydroelectric dams and only days after China's State Environmental Protection Administration had announced plans for drastic increases in water prices to curb demand. "Despite severe shortages, water is still too cheap to be used economically," said the administration's vice-director, Wang Jirong. Drought-hit megacities like Beijing and Tianjin were first in line for price hikes, he said. "This reform will ease the current water pressure of these beleaguered cities." Price rises would bolster promises by the Yellow River Conservancy Commission to cut consumption of the river's water for irrigation by 10 percent.

Nobody was talking of calling off the south-north project. But the myth that all the country's water problems would be solved once Yangtze water was flowing into the Yellow River seemed to have been broken. The last country to embrace unflinchingly the doctrine of the conquest of nature and the desire to remake its geography at will seemed finally to have accepted that enough was enough. We shall see what happens in practice. But as I read these stories, I received an e-mail from an Indian architect returned from two months in China learning about the country's huge new investments in rainwater harvesting in Gansu. More than 2 million concrete water cellars were boosting farm yields across a wide area of near-desert. "I am very excited about the prospects for cooperation between India and China on this," he wrote. The new thinking, the soft engineering, was starting to happen on a scale that really made a difference.

On a ridge near the headquarters of the Yellow River Conservancy Commission at Zhengzhou, 450 miles west of Beijing, stands a giant statue of the mythical emperor Yu. He towers above the floodplain of the great waterway of northern China. One hand is outstretched, bestowing prosperity on his people. The other hand carries the tools with which the Chinese first raised dykes and dug irrigation canals in the valley 4,000 years ago. His face scowls defiantly toward the river. Taming it has been a grim, remorseless task. But maybe his successors are about to wipe the scowl off his face.

Maybe there is a better way.

FURTHER READINGS

Much of this book is based on interviews with engineers, scientists, and policy-makers in many countries, coupled with their internal documents. But below is a range of written sources that should be more widely available.

INTRODUCTION

Beaumont, P., M. Bonine, and K. McLachlan (eds.). (1989). *Qanat, Kariz, and Khettara*. Wisbech, UK: Menas Press.

Issar, A.S. (1985). *Water Shall Flow from the Rock*. Berlin: Springer-Verlag.

CHAPTER ONE

Shapiro, J. (2001). *Mao's War Against Nature*. Cambridge, UK: Cambridge University Press.

Wang, S. (2002). *Resource-Oriented Water Management*. Beijing: China Water Power Press.

CHAPTER TWO

Goldsmith, E., and N. Hildyard. (1984). *The Social and Environmental Effects of Large Dams*. San Francisco: Sierra Club.

World Commission on Dams. (2000). *Dams and Development*. London: Earthscan.

CHAPTER THREE

Collins, R.O. (2002). *The Nile*. New Haven, CT: Yale University Press.

Howell, P.P., and J.A. Allan. (1994). *The Nile: Sharing a Scarce Resource*. Cambridge, UK: Cambridge University Press.

CHAPTER FOUR

Adams, W.M. (1992). *Wasting the Rain*. London: Earthscan.

Hollis, G.E. et al. (1993). *The Hadejia-Nguru Wetlands*. Geneva: IUCN.

CHAPTER FIVE

McCully, P. (1996). *Silenced Rivers*. London: Zed Books.

Paranjpye, V. (1988). *Evaluating the Tehri Dam*. New Delhi, India: Indian National Trust for Art and Cultural Heritage (INTACH).

CHAPTER SIX

Anon. (1989). *The Great Man-Made River Project*. Tripoli, Libya: Management and Implementation Authority of the Great Man-Made River Project.

CHAPTER SEVEN

Postel, S. (1999). *Pillar of Sand: Can the Irrigation Miracle Last?* New York: W.W. Norton.

CHAPTER EIGHT

Smedley, P.L., and D.G. Kinniburgh. (2002). A Review of the Source, Behaviour, and Distribution of Arsenic in Natural Waters. *Applied Geochemistry* 17:517–68.

Susheela, A.K. (1995). *Epidemiological Studies of Health Risks from Drinking Water Naturally Contaminated with Fluoride*. Rome: International Association of Hydrological Studies.

CHAPTER NINE

Lindahl, K. (ed.). (1999). *Alleviating the Consequences of an Ecological Catastrophe*. Stockholm: Swedish UNIFEM Committee.

Reznichenko, G. (1992). *The Aral Sea Tragedy*. Moscow: Novoyti.

CHAPTER TEN

Artemis, C. (2003). *Development of Water Resources in Cyprus*. Nicosia: Water Development Department, Government of Cyprus.

CHAPTER ELEVEN

Beaumont, P., M. Bonine, and K. McLachlan (eds). (1989). *Qanat, Kariz, and Khettara*. Wisbech, UK: Menas Press.

CHAPTER TWELVE

Agarwal, A., and S. Natrain. (1997). *Dying Wisdom*. New Delhi, India: Centre for Science and Environment.

Oweis, T. et al. (eds.). (2004). *Indigenous Water-Harvesting Systems in West Asia and North Africa*. Aleppo, Syria: International Center for Agricultural Research in the Dry Areas.

CHAPTER THIRTEEN

Nabhan, G.P. (1986). Papago Indian Desert Agriculture and Water Control in the Sonoran Dester, 1697–1934. *Applied Geography* 6:43–59.

CHAPTER FOURTEEN

Shah, T. (2003). Sustaining Asia's Groundwater Boom. *Natural Resources Forum* 27:130–41.

Shah, T. (2000). Mobilizing Social Energy against Environment Change: Understanding the Groundwater Recharge Movement in India. *Natural Resources Forum* 24:197–209.

CHAPTER FIFTEEN

Tiffen, M. et al. (1994). *More People, Less Erosion*. Chichester, UK: John Wiley & Sons.

Reij, C., and A. Waters-Bayer. (2001). *Farmer Innovation in Africa*. London: Earthscan.

CHAPTER SIXTEEN

Postel, S. (1999). *Pillar of Sand: Can the Irrigation Miracle Last?* New York: W.W. Norton.

CHAPTER SEVENTEEN

FogQuest (http://www.fogquest.org).
Seawater Greenhouse (http://www.seawatergreenhouse.com/).

CHAPTER EIGHTEEN

Acreman, M.C., and G.E. Hollis. (1996). *Water Management and Wetlands in Sub-Saharan Africa.* Geneva: IUCN.

Loth, P. (ed.). (2004). *The Return of the Water: Restoring the Waza Logone Floodplain in Cameroon.* Geneva: IUCN.

UNESCO. (2003). *Water for People, Water for Life.* New York: U.N. World Water Development Report; New York: Berghahn Books.

Willcocks, Sir W. (1984). *Ancient System of Irrigation in Bengal.* Delhi, India: BR Publishing.

CHAPTER NINETEEN

Cunningham, S. (2002). *The Restoration Economy.* San Francisco: Berrett-Koehler.

Schwartz, D. (1997). *Delta.* London: Thames and Hudson.

Thesiger, W. (1964). *The Marsh Arabs.* London: Longmans.

CHAPTER TWENTY

Barlow, M., and T. Clarge. (2002). *Blue Gold: The Battle against Corporate Threat of the World's Water.* Toronto: Stoddart.

International Consortium of Investigative Journalists. (2003). *The Water Barons.* Washington, D.C.: Public Integrity Books.

ACKNOWLEDGMENTS

This book is the product of more than a decade of research in numerous countries, carried out for a number of magazines and newspapers and, in the later stages, specifically for the book. So, many dozens of people have helped along the way. Some are acknowledged and cited in the text and I won't mention them again. Others would prefer anonymity. Still others, I fear, I have forgotten.

Of the rest, I should say thanks to several editors who have sent me around the world exploring water issues, often on the basis of little more than my fervently expressed hunch that a story would result. Bill O'Neill, first at *New Scientist* and later at the *Guardian* newspaper, is foremost among them. Without his support I wouldn't have made trips to Kenya, India, Bangladesh, Israel, and elsewhere. But thanks as well to Jeremy Webb; Stephanie Pain; Michael Kenward, who ignited many interests rehearsed here by letting me explore the River Colorado on *New Scientist*'s payroll; Alun Anderson, who sent me underground in Cyprus; and Ian Sample, who assigned me to Kyoto for the World Water Forum.

In addition, Bruce Stutz sent me to Nigeria to explore the crisis on the Hadejia-Nguru wetland; Robert Lamb and others at the CGIAR "Future

Harvest" network judged my work worthy of a journalism prize that funded the later stages of my researches; Don Hinrichsen, then at UNDP, got me to Karakalpakstan; and Mary Kelly of Environmental Defense took me down to the Rio Grande. In preparing this book, my editor Todd Baldwin at Island Press was critical in turning the parts into a coherent whole.

Many experts have given me their time and wisdom on water issues over the years. I cannot name them all, but this time I would especially like to thank Arie Issar in Israel, Tushaar Shah and Dipankar Chakraborti in India, plus Phil Williams and Paddy McCully at the International Rivers Network, along with Lester Brown, Nicholas Hildyard, Michael Mortimore, Sunita Narain, the late Ted Hollis, and, most important of all, the late Anil Agarwal—to whom this book is dedicated.

INDEX

Black Sea: 121
Blass, Symcha: 181–2, 184
Blue revolution: 188
Bolivia: 155, 235
Boutros-Ghali, Boutros: 42
Brahmaputra, River: 25, 85, 87, 96
British Geological Survey: 94, 190
Bucket-and-drip irrigation: 173–5, 184
Bucketwheel: 50–52
Burkina Faso: 148, 175–7, 195
Burma: 247
Burundi: 44

Calcutta: 78, 91, 219
California: 16, 33, 36, 56, 69, 71, 181–4, 186, 221, 227
Cambodia: 31, 37, 139, 143, 189
Cameroon: 213–4
Canada: 14, 16, 28, 71, 196–7
Canary Islands: 135, 199, 204
Caribbean: 26, 197, 200, 204
Caspian Sea: 19, 112, 121
Cauvery, River: 85, 87
Central African Republic: 246
Chad: 63, 75, 148, 214
Chad, Lake: 59, 63, 213–4
Chakraborti, Dipankar: 91, 95, 98
Chihuahua desert: 10, 191
Chile: 99, 106, 196–7
China:
    Ancient water use: 30
    Aquifers: 14, 36, 78, 99, 106, 135–7
    Aridification: 14
    Arsenic: 99
    Dams: 12, 34, 71, 73, 246–7
    Floods: 15, 248
    Fluoride: 106
    Irrigation practices: 20, 186, 188–9
    Rainwater harvesting: 185, 248
    South-North Transfer Project: 11–5, 17, 33–34, 37, 85, 122, 247–8
    Water demand: 86
    Water pricing: 239, 248
    See also Yellow and Yangtze Rivers
Chinampas: 158–9
Cloud seeding: 195
Cold War: 43–44, 53, 72, 195
Colombia: 156, 200
Colorado, River: 12, 16, 20, 112, 153, 191
Communal property and management: 141, 167, 175
Congo, Democratic Republic of: 246

Congo, River: 17, 28, 246
Consumption patterns: 9, 20–22, 26, 28, 90, 182, 188, 208, 237–9, 248
Contour bunding: 147, 175–8
Corn: see Maize
Cotton: 30, 45, 63, 110–20, 153, 164, 217–8, 237
Cotton, Arthur: 165–6
Cyprus: 125–35, 137

Dams:
    Alternatives and: 20, 146, 148, 178, 182, 186, 236, 241–6
    Check-dams: 162, 165, 174
    Destructive impacts: 18, 33–34, 48, 53, 55–63, 71, 87, 109–22, 212, 226–7
    Earthquake risks: 65–70
    General: 12–13, 70–73, 83, 161–2, 209, 211
    Mega-engineering: 16, 23, 41, 43–4, 85
    Removal: 34
    See also Hydroelectricity, Reservoirs, and individual dams
Danube, River: 17
Darcy's Law: 8
Delhi: 66, 85, 102–3, 105, 107, 240
Dhaka: 78, 89–91, 94
Dnieper, River: 121
Don, River: 121
Drinking water: 17, 36, 51, 72, 90, 92, 94, 98, 100–1
Drip irrigation: 20, 181–2, 184–6, 192, 236
Drought:
    Climate change: 18, 63
    Drought-proofing: 44–45, 55, 127, 137, 144, 156–8, 173, 176, 195, 243
    General: 26, 52, 59, 218, 247–8
    Man-made drought: 214
    Water conflicts: 87, 191–2
Dust storms: 14, 115

Earthquakes: 13, 65–71
Ecuador: 156, 197, 235
Eden Again Project: 224–6
Efficient use of water: 9, 19–21, 26, 54, 119, 141, 169–70, 183, 185–90, 193, 198, 202, 209, 212, 214, 236–7
Egypt:
    Ancient Egypt: 30, 41–42, 132, 139
    Aquifers: 75–76, 135
    Cold War, geopolitics and the Nile: 42–5, 50–4